HOW TO ENCOUNTER THE

DIRECTION

OF *God*

DR. PATTY SADALLAH

Encountering the DIRECTION of God

Experience Jesus Book 3

By Dr. Patty Sadallah

Printed in the Unites States of America

ISBN 979-8-9869158-0-7

All Scriptures in this book were found on Biblegateway.com and are in the AMP version unless otherwise indicated.

Published by IngramSpark www.IngramSpark.com

HOW TO ENCOUNTER THE

DIRECTION

OF *God*

DR. PATTY SADALLAH

Dedication

To To Kris,

For inspiring me with her radical obedience to God's Direction.

Table of Contents

Acknowledgments

My sincere thanks go out to the faithful Spirit Life Circle Members and others who participated in the HEALING book class that was used as a process for writing this book. And thank you to and to those who agreed to share their encounter stories or journal messages in this book: Kris Castro, Zac Schultz, Jeanette Chamberlin, Kathryn Lapp, Cindy Fiebig, my sister Michele McLaughlin, and my brother Dan MacInnis, retired Rear Admiral of the US Navy.

I'd like to thank my weekly faithful prayer partners, Katie Beckwith, and Larry Silver who also edited this book.

Thanks to Julie Sordi who made the beautiful lyric video collages for each chapter and to Tasha Markovich my wonderful collage photographer. And to every artist for whom we were blessed by their inspirational songs: Unspoken, Paul Baloche, Casting Crowns, Big Daddy Weave, Chris Tomlin, Francesca Battistelli, Sinach, Sidewalk Prophets, and Matthew West. I also appreciate the teaching influence and inspiration of Dr. Mark Virkler, Walt Pilcher, and Lance

Wallnau and the amazing contributions to Christian wisdom and understanding of the late C.S. Lewis and Hans Poley.

I am grateful for the talented filmmakers whose film clips are included: Making an Earthen Pot- Wild Films India, Know Me Here clip from The Chronicles of Narnia: The Voyage of the Dawn Treader- Andrew Anderson, Make me Lie Down in Green Pastures- Iroquois Valley Christian Church, Movie Trailer for Return to the Hiding Place- Peter C. Spencer, Tell your Story clip from King's Faith- Nicholas DiBella, Science Short: The Observer Effect- Jen Foxbit, Strangers film- Igniter Media, We are Here and Jo Jo Saves the Day clips from Horton Hears a Who- Blue Sky Studios, When Lambs become Lions clip from Robin Hood- Ridley Scott, and How to Speak in Tongues Part 1 and Part 2- Dr. Mark Virkler.

Thank you to my Fiverr.com resources; Matias Baldanza the book cover designer and Daiana Morales for the paperback and E-book formatting. Thank you to Kathy Jiamboi and Kristen Rosenstock for the gift of the beautiful series logos and the helpful guidance for the webpage updating.

And my husband George and daughters Jamael, Leah, and Noelle for their constant support. A special thanks to my sister, Michele McLaughlin, who is my biggest fan and gives my books away free to everyone she meets!

And last but by no means least, I would like to thank Jesus for showing up for each person as all these Names so faithfully!

You've Always Been by Unspoken

https://bit.ly/3kCslLp

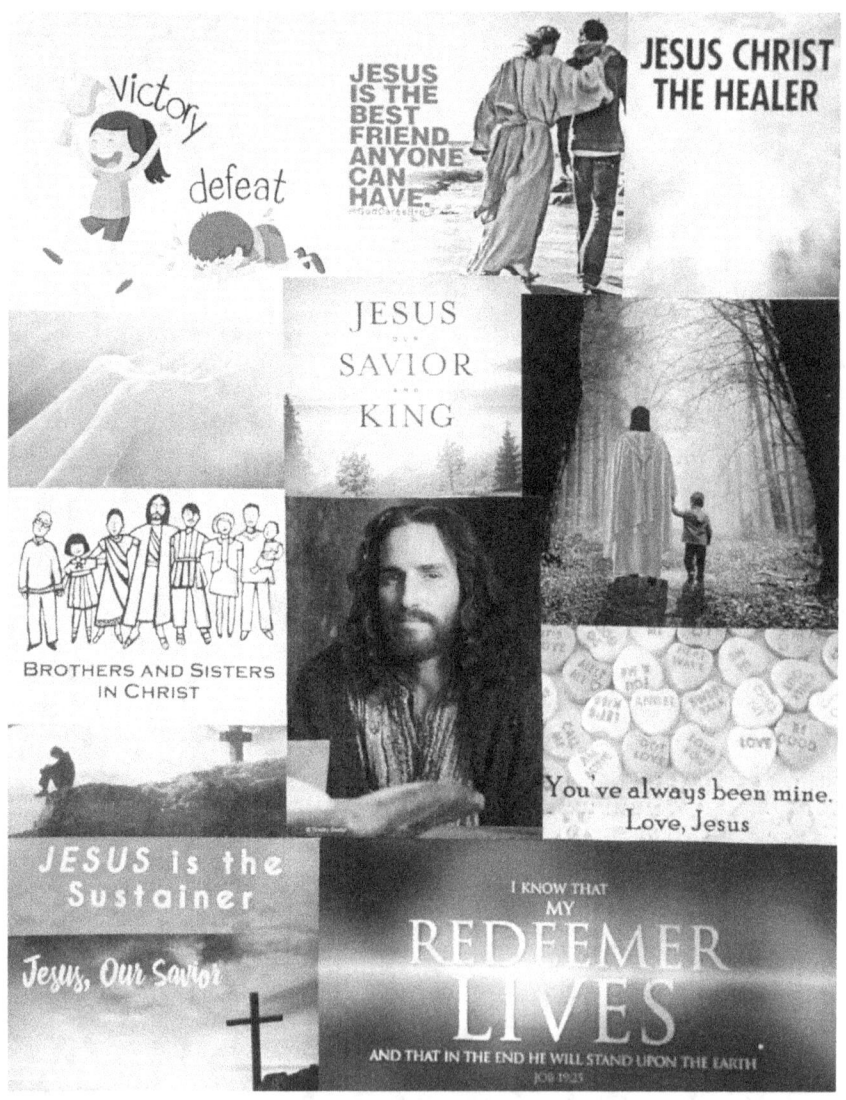

Experience Jesus
Series Introduction

*I*magine that God has His own TV channel. Just like others you might have at your fingertips. But unlike everything on your TV, His is supernatural. When we watch TV, it is a one-directional experience. You can see and emotionally connect with the programming on other channels as a distant observer. But the God channel is a two-way experience. You jump through the television and become part of God's action. This may seem like a strange idea to you, but essentially, this is the experience you will have with this book series. You will learn how to access God through the eyes and ears of your heart to connect with the various Names of Him directly.

John 10:27 "My sheep hear My voice, and I know them, and they follow Me."

One of the reasons Jesus died for us on the cross was to gain us direct access to the Father so we may know Him intimately one Name at a time.

Colossians 1:9-12 "[9]For this reason also, since the day we heard of it, we have not ceased to pray for you and to ask that you may be filled with the knowledge of His will in all spiritual wisdom and understanding, [10]so that you will walk in a manner worthy of the LORD, to please Him in all respects, bearing fruit in every good work and increasing in the knowledge of God; [11]strengthened with all power, according to His glorious might, for the attaining of all steadfastness and patience; joyously [12]giving thanks to the Father, who has qualified us to share in the inheritance of the saints in Light."

This book will guide you to experience Jesus yourself. Together, you will address your personal worries, health, family, future, and other life issues. Your experiences with God will move you beyond your limiting beliefs and you will learn how to align yourself with His perfect will for your life.

Why God's Names

The Names of God are personal and powerful. Names like Bridegroom, Mighty Counselor, Friend, Defender, Supernatural Provider, and Healer are intimate for a reason. Would you marry, seek counseling, trust with your secrets or your health, or lean on in times of crisis someone you can't see, hear, or feel? God was called these Names because He personally showed up for people in these ways in the days of the Bible. He is even more able to do that for you today!

While researching my last book, I was astonished that the original manuscripts of the Bible contain 950 Names of God. This reference will help you see them in their scriptural contexts. https://bit.ly/313CAiR[1]

---

[1] https://christiananswers.net/dictionary/namesofgod.html 950 Names and Titles of God

Unfortunately, in our English Bible translations, we don't see all these distinctive Names because the English language does not have words to make those distinctions. But they exist, in the Greek, Hebrew, Aramaic, and Latin texts.

In Bible times, people encountered God in a variety of different ways and then named Him for those experiences. Here is an example from the Bible when Hagar met God personally and gave Him a Name.

Genesis 16:11-13 (NOG) [11] Then the Messenger of Yahweh said to her,

"You are pregnant,
   and you will give birth to a son.
You will name him Ishmael [God Hears],
   because Yahweh has heard your cry of distress.
[12] He will be as free and wild as an untamed donkey.
He will fight with everyone, and everyone will fight with him.
He will have conflicts with all his relatives." [a]
[13] Hagar named Yahweh, who had been speaking to her, "You Are **El Roi**." She said, "This is the place where I watched the one who watches over me."

The "Messenger of Yahweh" was the pre-incarnate Jesus. Anytime you see the word *"the"* before the word "angel" of the Lord, or in this translation, "messenger," it is referencing the pre-incarnate Jesus. Hagar knew that she was personally encountering God. She named Him *El Roi.* **El** is another word for Yahweh, which means the complete fullness of God. She added the word **Roi** to mean "the God who sees me and watches over me." Hagar had met the Omnipresence of God in a personal way.

It was because she experienced what God did for her that she gave Him this Name. Early in my doctoral journey, the Lord helped me understand more about the importance of encountering God's Names.

Knowing about vs. Knowing[23]

I was meditating on a verse in Titus about the notion of people claiming to know God, but it not showing in their behavior.

Titus 1:16a, They claim to know God, but by their actions they deny Him.

I asked Jesus to show me the difference between someone who thinks they know You and someone who really knows You. (Note that Jesus' voice will always appear indented and in *italics* so it can be easily identified.)

*The difference is one knows **about** Me, and the other **knows Me intimately**. Let Me show you what I mean.*

Jesus showed me a man in the desert. He had chapped lips and a distressed look on his face. He frantically looked and thought he saw water. But as he kept walking, he realized that it was only a mirage.

³ Excerpt from Just ask Jesus Book 1 Series Introduction of *How to Live a Worry-Free* Life by Dr. Patty Sadallah, pp. 26-28.

There was no real water, only something that looked like water. It's good to know what water looks like. It's better to be able to drink some when you are thirsty!

*To learn about Me is like showing a hungry and thirsty man a picture of a magnificent banquet but there is nothing to eat or drink. Seeing the picture may bring some benefits, but he is left ultimately unsatisfied. The actual need is unfulfilled. This is what it is like to only learn **about** Me.*

*The spiritual need to **know** Me is even stronger than that man's physical need for water. A mirage is an illusion; a trick of the eye caused by light refraction and heat waves. Knowing only about Me is a trick too. But it doesn't fool the soul. The soul knows its need for the True God.*

To truly satisfy the hunger and thirst in your soul, you must drink deeply of the Living Water. Water is refreshing, rejuvenating, and restores more than you can see and feel. Come and drink deeply the Living Water. You must eat the food of My Presence. You must enter the Holy of Holies where you can encounter My Presence. I have gained you direct access to the Father by way of the indwelling Holy Spirit by My work on the cross. Do not neglect this privilege.

This is accomplished by you spending time with Me. Consider John 17:3 "This is eternal life, that they may know You, the only true God, and Jesus Christ whom You have sent." To know someone is an intimate thing. To know of something or someone implies knowledge from a distance. It is not My desire for you to know Me distantly or haphazardly in a third-party sort of way as in only through the work of a pastor or a preacher.

You cannot know Me without personally drawing close to Me. It is through steady communion with Me; Father, Son, and Holy Spirit that you will truly Know Me. And knowing leads to trusting, believing, and obeying which are fruits of the eternal life you now have.

It's just like knowing anyone personally. To trust someone, I need to spend time with them to learn who they are and if I can rely on them. After some time, if I feel safe, I tend to want to spend more time and then come to trust them. I spend the most time with people that I like to be around; people who build me up, encourage me, and show me love. No one does that better than You, LORD!"

Yes. The difference between knowing in your head and surrendering in your heart is clarified in James 2:19 'You believe that God is one. You do well; the demons also believe, and shudder.' The demons know who I AM, of course. But they do not accept and surrender to Me and have no intimate relationship with Me. This is an important distinction. Remember, I live in your heart, not in your head.

Yes. LORD. I can see the difference.

Every time you take a drink today, spend time reflecting on the Living Water and come and fellowship with Me. Tune to Me in the quiet and listen for My voice. Seek Me and you will find Me. Spend time getting to know Me. Ask Me to show you things. I certainly have a lot to show you! It's My heart's desire to spend time with you too! Communing with Me is the only way for your spiritual hunger and thirst to be satisfied. This is how you truly know Me!

Encountering the Realness of God

I was listening to the dramatized radio version of C.S. Lewis's *The Screwtape Letters*[ii] by Focus on the Family in my car and came to Letter 31. In this last chapter of the book, the Lord grabbed my attention, and I flushed with Glory bumps.

C.S. Lewis wrote the now-classic *Screwtape Letters* in 1942 amidst WWII. It is a fictionalized story that teaches spiritual warfare in reverse. Screwtape is an experienced demon who is counseling his nephew, Wormwood, a new temper assigned to a "patient," much like a guardian angel for the opposite side. Wormwood's job is to speak lies into his patient's ears to keep him away from God's plans and ensure that he stays well below the calling that God (the Enemy as the demons call Him) has for him.

There are 31 letters that Screwtape writes to Wormwood, and each teaches the lies that the enemy speaks into our lives to throw us off our Christian impact. The entire book and dramatized recording are amazing, but what really got my attention was Letter 31!

Here is a list of quoted snippets from this letter that will hopefully shed light on the relevance of what we are doing here in this book series. Screwtape is looking for Wormwood to take him for his punishment for failing with his patient. He goes on a rant about what Wormwood did that lost this patient to the other side for good:

"All our efforts are dismayed...How well I know the instant that they snatched him from us! Did you see it for yourself? ...There was a sudden change in his eyes as he saw you (Wormwood) for the first time, and he recognized the part you had had in him and knew that you had it no longer! ....It was as if he shed for good the all-wet clinging garments that held him back and was completely cleansed....

He went so easily! It was sheer instantaneous liberation! Did you mark how, as if he was born for it, the little vermin entered the new life? How all his doubts like in the twinkling of an eye became ridiculous!'...

Do you know what your fatal flaw was? When he saw you, he also saw HIM... You allowed him to see that HE is REAL. ... He, to them, is clarity itself. And worse yet, He was in the form of a MAN! The one for whom he thought was dead is ALIVE and even now at his door! ... All our efforts are dismayed!"[4]

Nothing can stop you when you see Him as **real** and for you now. He is at your door. Meet Him, and you will be free, healed, and transformed into the best version of yourself!

Why we Picture Jesus

The three Persons of the Trinity all play a role in the encountering experience. It is ultimately the **Father** who desires that you commune with Him while seeing and speaking with **Jesus** by the power of the **Holy Spirit**. Jesus is the only person of the Trinity that we can honestly imagine. He was a man like us, and that makes Him accessible and understandable as a person. The Father needs the Perfection of Jesus for us to be able to come near to Him. When the Father looks at you, He sees Jesus covering you with His Perfection. The Power to do this is accomplished by the indwelling Holy Spirit, who is God's very essence inside of every believer. This privilege was accomplished by Jesus's work on the cross.

> Genesis 1:1 (NOG) says [1] In the beginning, **Elohim** created heaven and earth. [2] The earth was formless and empty, and darkness covered the deep water. The **Ruach Elohim** was hovering over the water. [3] Then **Elohim** said, «Let there be light!" So there was light.

Elohim is the plural word for a singular God. You see in this verse that the self-existent **Father God** conceives of the Heavens and the Earth. **Jesus, also called the Word**, speaks this conception into

---

[4] Focus on the Family Radio Theatre Collector's Edition; The Screwtape Letters by CS Lewis @2009 Tyndale House Publishers. (Snippets from Letter 31)

existence, and the **Ruach Elohim**, who is the Holy Spirit is the power that manifests it into reality.

So, even though you will be connecting with Jesus, know that you are really engaging with Elohim, the Triune God. There will be more on how this works in the Creator Chapter of *How to Encounter the POWER of God: Experience Jesus Book 4.*

Jesus Himself instructs us to encounter the Father God by fixing our eyes on Him. He is the relatable third of the Trinity.

> John 14:7-9 [7] If you had [really] known Me, you would also have known My Father. From now on, you know Him and have seen Him."
>
> [8] Philip said to Him, "Lord, show us the Father, and then we will be satisfied." [9] Jesus said to him, "Have I been with you for so long a time, and you do not know Me yet, Philip, nor recognize clearly who I am? Anyone who has seen Me has seen the Father. How can you say, 'Show us the Father?'

Meet God and Get to Know Yourself

Perhaps one of the most important benefits of the ***Experience Jesus*** series is that you meet your true self in meeting Him. Referencing the Screwtape Letters again, in one of his earliest letters, Screwtape councils Wormwood that God's strategy is to help people realize that He created them uniquely and distinctly. The Devil's strategy is to have people drift away from their uniquely created selves and become like everyone else. Screwtape shares with Wormwood:

"When He talks of their losing their selves, He only means abandoning the clamor of self-will; once they have done that, He really gives them back all their personality and boasts (I'm afraid, sincerely) that when they are wholly His, they will be more themselves than ever."[5]

---

[5] Focus on the Family Radio Theatre Collector's Edition; The Screwtape Letters by CS Lewis

Consequently, Screwtape continues to advise on how to sweep Christians away with groupthink, popular self-centered notions that lead them farther away from understanding their unique giftings and purposes.

God knows you even better than you know yourself. He truly wants you to see yourself through His eyes. This is part of your journey in this series. As you meet Him and better understand the fullness of His Identity, you meet yourself and discover your Christ Identity, the ideal version of you that He sees you as already.

We can call on God by any of His Names that make Him real to us at the moment and learn directly from Him how to pray with authority for the victories we need in life. Mike Noble from the Cleveland House of Prayer calls God the "trillion faceted diamond." He often asks people which facet(s) pierced their hearts. Some have met the Provider and can trust Him with their provisional needs but don't know Him as their Friend. Others have met the Great Physician and trust God with their physical needs but not their emotional ones.

Our God is ALL those things and so much more. He wants you to allow more and more facets of the diamond to pierce your heart and transform you. He wants you to be free, whole, and victorious.

Galatians 5:25 says, "If we live by the Spirit, let us also walk by the Spirit."

It's Normal

God created everyone to see and hear Him with the eyes and ears of their heart. If you were unable to do so, you would never be able

---

to close your eyes and picture a memory or hear in your mind a conversation you had or remember what you heard or saw in a film. The screen of your mind gives you the ability to see, hear, and feel things. God created the eyes and ears of your heart, most importantly for you to connect with Him. In fact, without the eyes and ears of your heart, you never would have accepted Him as your Savior in the first place. God is not willing for any to perish, so He wired us to be able to communicate with Him.

2 Peter 3:9 "The Lord does not delay [as though He were unable to act] and is not slow about His promise, as some count slowness, but is [extraordinarily] patient toward you, not wishing for any to perish but for all to come to repentance."

The entire Bible was written with the same four keys that you will use to encounter God. Two-thirds of the Bible was written through the "ears of the heart" as the human messengers wrote down what they heard straight from the Lord. The other third was written through the "eyes of the heart" as dreams and visions from the Lord were carefully recorded.

God was communicating messages from heaven. He is the same yesterday, today, and forever (Hebrews 13:8). SO, if this is how God spoke to people in the days of the writing of the Bible, He surely can do it now! And even more so now that Christians have the indwelling Holy Spirit whose job it is to fill us with the power to connect with God's Nature and release His Love to others. This direct access to Father God is what Jesus accomplished for us on the cross.

Why the Special Place

In your first encounter that you will have in the next chapter, you will be taken to the **Special Place.** This is for you and Jesus privately. For some, it may be a beautiful location that brings them fond memories of the past. For others, it is a lovely place that they have never seen before. Jesus knows where your special place is, so do not try to figure that out or tell Him where it is. Just let yourself go wherever the Lord takes you.

The special place is essential because once you have seen Jesus there once, you can easily imagine going there again. You can expect to see Him there whenever you need.

He is not limited by this location. When you meet Him there, He can take you anywhere! Some of our encounters will not begin at the special place for specific reasons that will make sense. But I want you to get familiar with having a spiritual home base. Look around, and see more of it as you go back for more experiences. The more you look, the more it will expand.

When I first saw my special place, it was no more than a back porch and a small grassy knoll. It has grown to include a flower path to the sea, a picturesque river and waterfall, a gazebo, a swing set, a dancefloor, and a unique tree. After two years and many adventures with Jesus in my special place, I got to see this place in the natural world in Israel. It was a short walk to the Sea of Galilee! It was incredible. I believe that many places on Earth are shadows of real majestic places in heaven. It was astonishing when I saw the similarities of my photos of that place to the descriptions I had written about it years before!

Jesus can take you anywhere once you begin. Not all your encounters on this journey will start in your special place. However, the more comfortable you are going there, the quicker you can meet Him, even if you are amid chaos or a crisis.

Film Clips, Lyric Videos, and Collages

The Lord is creative. He wants to use as many aspects of the language of the heart to connect with you as possible. God has used media to communicate in each book that He has written through me. This time, the Lord wanted beautiful collages of our chapter lyric videos as a way for you to meditate on the words and connect even more with the songs as a way to ponder on them personally with the Lord. As beautiful as they are in the book, you really must see them in color! Here is a link to all of them in color in addition to all media links in this book.

It is amazing to me how much more can be said in a song verse than can be said in pages of a book. The Lord wants you to exercise the eyes and ears of your heart in a variety of ways to strengthen them. Like physical muscles, the more you use them, the stronger they get.

Keep this webpage open so you can simply click to the next media link in the book to watch, listen and experience everything without missing a beat! Website: www.PattySadallah.com/Experience-Jesus.

God's Heart for You

The capacity to believe in Me is enlarged tremendously by experiencing Me! You encounter the Truth of who I AM to you personally, today, yesterday, and tomorrow when you fix your eyes on Me in all areas. I am sufficient for all of your needs. (see 2 Corinthians 12:9)

When you encounter Me by My Names personally, you begin to collect memories of Me being Who you need for each circumstance. This is how you will live your gospel story in the world and represent Me confidently. The more you encounter Me in these daily, personal ways, the more you give Me access to your heart for transformation.

Every name I have been for others in the Bible, I can be for you. Won't you allow Me to be them for you?

The Gospel is nothing more than a personal recounting of what you have seen, heard, and experienced of God directly. When you encounter Me personally, you are a witness of the REAL God. Memories you collect with Me will increase your trust, faith, belief, and boldness to represent Me well in the world. The more you encounter the different aspects of Me, the more confidence you will have that I AM who I say I AM. The more confidence you have, the more you will inspire others to trust Me. Make them want what you have in Me.

Tell your story. Your story is your living gospel, your record of what I have done in your life. Share every character and aspect of Me you have ever met. Introduce people to Me as the Provider, Healer, Shepherd, Defender, Savior, Counselor, Friend, Waymaker, Creator, etc. so they can know Me likewise.

*I am ready and waiting to meet you in these encounters. I am one God with many facets, way too large for anyone to understand completely. So, meet Me one Name at a time and build memories of personal times when you and I work through challenges and experienced joy together. The more you encounter Me, the easier it will be to Trust Me and believe in Me in all areas of life. I Am the **Promise Keeper**. You'll see!*

The Names Addressed in Each Book
Book 1: How to Encounter the *LOVE* of God

1. When you meet the **Heavenly Father,** you are introduced to the power of child-like faith and its mysterious ability to help

you connect with God purely and without the barriers to faith that adulthood brings.

2. When you meet the **Savior**, you learn in a most personal way, why the Lord chose to come as a human and died for YOU. You will understand the price paid for your salvation and why you were worth the cost to God. You will also appreciate the great exchange and the benefits that are yours now and forever as your inheritance.

3. When you meet **Immanuel,** you will encounter the God who always was, is, and always will be with you. He will show you that in an instant, you can see and feel His Covering and connect with His Mind, Will, and Emotion to handle any circumstance your days can bring.

4. When you meet the **Bridegroom,** you will understand the intimacy and value of God's genuine trust and partnership in your life. You will learn the benefits of being united to the All-powerful, All-knowing, All-benevolent, and Ever-Present God.

5. When you meet the **Friend,** you will encounter the joy of God as you have playful adventures with the One you trust with your heart, secrets, and life. You will learn about the powerful favor anointing that comes with the likeability factor of friendship and the role that praise and worship have in it.

Book 2: How to Encounter the *HEALING* of God

1. When you meet the **Great Physician,** He will show you the pathway to vibrant and abundant life. You will learn how to tune to Him for clarity on all conditions that need to be met for

physical healing and the relationship to spiritual, emotional, and mental health.

2. When you meet the **Comforter,** you will find the way to the peace that surpasses understanding by addressing past heart wounds and allowing Him to help you find forgiveness and give you a new heart.

3. When you meet the **Mighty Counselor,** you will learn how to spot the lies that keep you in bondage and trust God for the Truth that will set you free. Wisdom and understanding are found when you learn how to see your circumstances through God's eyes, ears, mind, and heart.

4. When you meet the **Deliverer,** He will show you the way to find freedom from bondages by standing on His authority and exercising the authority you have by His power to live according to His promises.

5. When you meet the **Miracle Worker,** He will show you key principles for determining His will and accessing His power to pull miracles down from heaven according to His promises.

Book 3: How to Encounter the *DIRECTION* of God

1. When you meet the **Truth,** He will guide you to clarity, wisdom, and understanding by interpreting scripture promises as they relate to your personal calling.

2. When you meet the **Shepherd,** you will see His gentle care, guidance, and protection as you learn to surrender your will and ways to His more perfect plan for you.

3. When you meet the **Author of your Story,** He will show you how to stay aligned to the ideal life plan that He has for you one day at a time.

4. When you meet the **Waymaker,** He will show you how He is working on your behalf often behind the scenes and without your awareness to equip you to accomplish your Kingdom purposes.

5. When you meet the **Supernatural Provider,** He will show you to look beyond natural limitations for accomplishing your work for God. You will encounter His limitlessness and exercise your authority to receive supernatural provisions for your Kingdom purposes.

Book 4: How to Encounter the *POWER* of God

1. When you meet the **Creator,** you will encounter the complexity and wonder of God and learn about the power of His spoken Word to create. Likewise, how you are made in His image to create as well.

2. When you meet **Almighty God,** you will encounter the Sovereign King of kings and get a greater sense of His Omni-Truths up close and personally. Limiting notions of God will be cast away.

3. When you meet **Defender,** God will show up as the one who fights on your behalf either on the spiritual warfare battlefield or in the Courts of Heaven. You will learn how and why you can access the defense of God in your everyday life.

4. When you meet the **Holy Spirit,** you will learn how to tap into the internal power of the Holy Spirit to live your most effective life without fears or limitations.

5. When you meet the **Lord of Hosts,** He will show you the angelic realm as its leader and teach you how to cooperate with the ministries of the angels assigned to protect and aid you throughout your life.

The Same Love by Paul Baloche

https://bit.ly/3gR8vtx

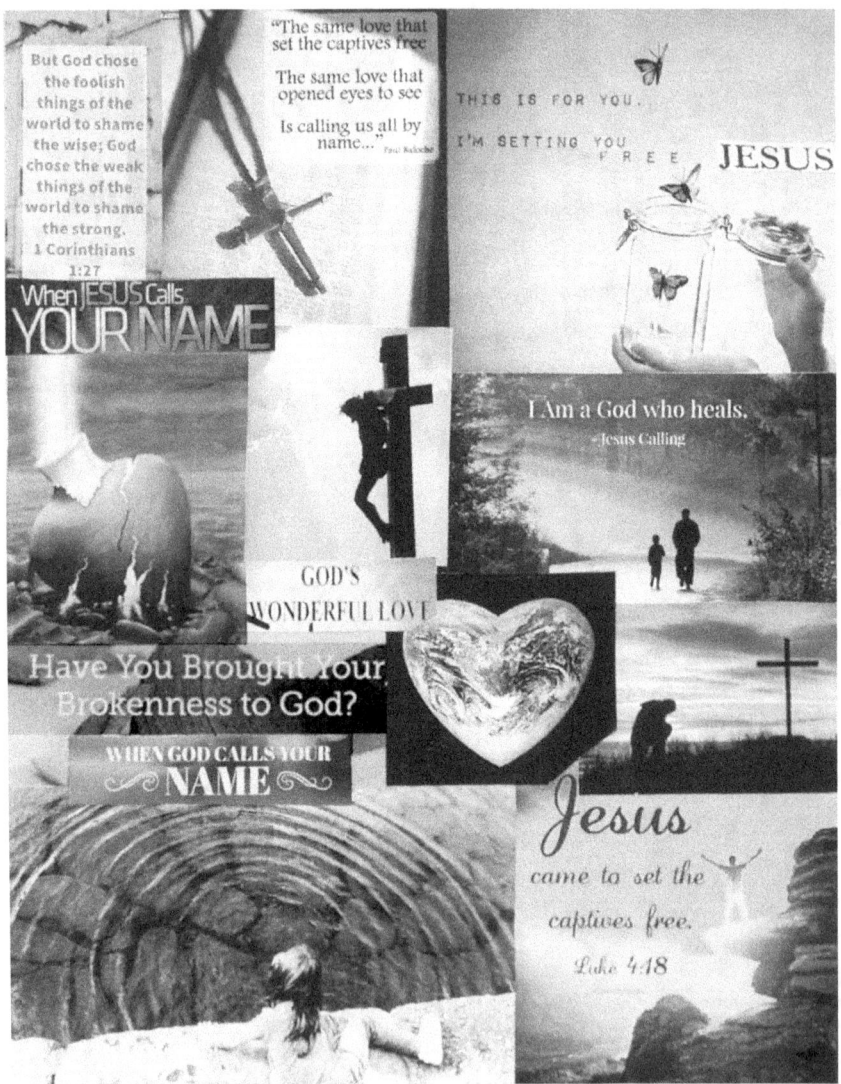

How to Encounter God

⌘

The conversations and adventures that you will have in this book are real spiritual encounters. They are not figments of your imagination. Believing this is the first step to having meaningful experiences with God.

By way of preparation for this journey, get yourself a journal. It can be as simple as a spiral-bound notebook, or as I love to use, one that has Scripture verses at the bottom of every page. I have noticed when I use this kind of journal, that often exactly what Jesus or I am saying on the journal page is reinforced by the Scripture on that page. God is so cool like that!

This is your personal journey. God will call you by name. In fact, He may even give you a new pet name that no one else has ever called you. Stick with this, and I pray that Jesus will meet you one Name at a time exactly where you need Him. I don't know anyone who has encountered the **realness** of Jesus that has not been changed.

If you have not accepted Jesus as your LORD and Savior, this is an important step for you to work through. Appendix B has a special salvation prayer where you can dedicate or re-dedicate your life to

Jesus. We will cover this issue extensively when you Meet the Savior chapter of How to Encounter the LOVE of God: Experience Jesus Book 1. He will seal this heart decision for all eternity so you can be assured of your salvation.

Finding God's Channel

The language of the heart is pictures, stories, music, emotions, and metaphors. Jesus demonstrated this by teaching through parables and stories relevant to the culture to connect with the hearts of the people at the time. The language of our heads is analytical and logical. Jesus reflected the character of His Father perfectly using the language of the heart. He spoke in the vernacular of their culture using common images of their day. He does the same thing today as you will see from the experiences that you, and all those for whom God has revealed Himself in this book series. You will learn how to tap into God's channel by putting your brain into the alpha state.

Alpha Brain Waves

Brain waves are measured by frequency, which is cycles per second, or hertz (Hz). They range from very slow to very fast. Alpha waves (8-12 Hz) fit in the middle of the spectrum, between beta and theta waves. Alpha is a state of alert relaxation and fosters creativity. Children from the age of 2 to 8 live primarily in the alpha brain state. They are too young to worry and simply go with the flow of life with play and creative imagination. [6]

Your brain produces alpha waves when you are not concentrating on anything in particular. For example, when you are driving and

---

[6] https://blog.mindvalley.com/science-behind-brainwaves/

realize that your mind has been wandering, but you are still able to keep your eyes on the road, you are in alpha.

In the Heavenly Father chapter of Book 1, you realize the importance of approaching God as a child as it naturally connects you with the alpha state and brings the faith of a child. We meet this Name of God first because it is crucial always to meet Him as a child. It took me about two years to realize how important this is to connect with God more effectively.

The alpha brain wave is one of the factors that help you tune into God's channel. You can easily learn the skill of putting your brain in alpha. In fact, the Dialogue Journaling tool we use to encounter God does just that! When your brain is producing these waves as part of your encountering experiences with Jesus, the results can reduce your stress levels and help you feel calmer, more loved, and most importantly, closer to a personal God.

Theta is the brain wave of logical thinking. Most adults spend their waking hours in theta. The brain wave looks more like an active lie detector with fast ups and downs, whereas the alpha state appears as slower rolling hills.

Biblical Meditation

The Bible includes 20 verses to encourage us to meditate on the Word.

> Psalm 104: [34] *May my meditation be pleasing to Him, as I rejoice in the LORD.*

Meditation is a heart posture whereby you surrender all the faculties of your brain to the Lord to gain His wisdom and insight. Wait, doesn't this seem like the stuff that the new agers do? Isn't meditation their word? Sure, but it was God's word first. Do you know why no one counterfeits a three-dollar bill? It is because there is no real $3.00 bill, and it's not a valuable number. The enemy is a counterfeiter. If the new agers are doing it, then something about it is a bit off and was swindled from what is real and valuable.

Let's look at the differences: New Agers seek to connect with the spirit realm when they meditate. They also relax to put their brains into an alpha state. But they seek to connect with spirits in general. We aim to connect with Jesus. This is an important distinction.

Matthew 7:9-11 ⁹ Or what man is there among you who, if his son asks for bread, will [instead] give him a stone? ¹⁰ Or if he asks for a fish, will [instead] give him a snake? ¹¹ If you then, evil (sinful by nature) as you are, know how to give good and advantageous gifts to your children, how much more will your Father who is in heaven [perfect as He is] give what is good and advantageous to those who keep on asking Him.

The Word promises that if you ask for Jesus, you get Jesus. If you ask for generalized spirits, the enemy will surely oblige. Never seek to speak or pray to dead family members or anyone other than God when meditating. The Strong's Exhaustive Concordance defines meditation: "to murmur; to converse with oneself, and hence aloud; speak; talk; babbling; communication; mutter; roar; mourn; a murmuring sound; a musical notation; to study; to ponder; revolve in your mind; imagine; pray; prayer; reflection; devotion.⁷ It is a surrender of your entire mind to God's Spirit to meditate on Him. The left-brained activities include reason, written language, and speech. The right-brained activities are related to music, art awareness, intuition, and imagination.

---

⁷ https://Biblehub.com/hebrew/yehgeh_1897.htm search word Strongs Concordance for "meditation"

You have all these characteristics included if you look at the meditation definition through the filter of all the left- and right activities of the brain.

Dialogue Journaling

We will be using dialogue journaling as our primary tool for connecting with God. Dr. Mark Virkler came up with four simple keys to hearing God's voice[8] for more than 11 years an unrelenting heart desire to commune with God personally. This simple statement summarizes the four keys: Hearing from God is as simple as 1) quieting yourself down, 2) fixing your eyes on Jesus, 3) tuning to spontaneity, and 4) writing it down. These are the steps for what Virkler calls the skill of dialogue journaling or two-way journaling.

1. **Quiet yourself down**- externally and internally

2. **Fix your Eyes on Jesus**- ask and expect to see, hear, and feel from Him

3. **Tune to spontaneity**- allow the pictures, thoughts, and feelings to bubble up without self-effort.

4. **Write down** what you saw, heard, felt, and thought.

The entire Bible was written by God speaking or showing someone something spontaneously and then writing it down so others could read it. Habakkuk 2:1-2 demonstrates these steps beautifully. Habakkuk was a prophet at the time when the Lord was exiling the Jews to other nations for what would be 70 years. The prophet was perplexed by why the Israelites were being taken away and wanted to talk to God about it. The four key steps are revealed in Habakkuk 2:1-2:

---

[8] *4 Keys to Hearing God's Voice* by Drs Mark and Patti Virkler, CWG Ministries,

Verse segment/ **How it relates to the Four Keys**

> [1] *I will stand on my guard post and station myself on the rampart;* / Habakkuk found a quiet place so he could look up to God. He was posturing his heart to speak to God Himself.

And I will keep watch to see what He will speak to me,/

He was looking and listening with an expectation to hear from God personally, using the eyes and ears of his heart.

> *And how I may reply when I am reproved./* Habakkuk knew it would be a conversation with God. He knew that he could hear what God had to say AND that he could reply to God.
>
> [2]*Then the LORD answered me and said,/* God did reply personally.
>
> *"Record the vision and inscribe it on tablets, so the one who reads it may run."/* God commanded Habakkuk to write down what He was saying. Writing it down is not just for you to remember, but it can also become a blessing for others.

Managing Expectations

Your first exercise will help you with all future exercises. God will take you to your *special place* where you and He will have your first encounter. Your conversations and adventures can begin in this place and Jesus can take you anywhere He wants from there. Getting familiar with your spiritual place will help you comfortably anchor your memories with Jesus. The more you go there, the more He will expand it so you can see and experience more there.

Before we begin, I wanted to manage some expectations. God's voice does not sound like an external, booming, or roaring voice. As we have already learned, it sounds like your own thoughts, pictures, emotions, and songs but is spontaneous with God's character and nature. So, don't jam the receiver with unrealistic expectations that a James Earl Jones-esque voice needs to be speaking in an audible voice for it to be God.

Let's practice using the eyes and ears of the heart right now. Wherever you are, close your eyes. If you are in your bedroom, picture your kitchen or another room in your house. "Look" on the screen of your mind and scan the room. Notice the details that you see. They may not be as clear as if your eyes were open looking at that room, but I'm willing to bet that you have clear impressions in your mind of those rooms. You were just using the eyes of your heart.

Now, close your eyes and begin to sing the Happy Birthday song in your mind. Hear it? That's you using the ears of your heart. If you could hear and see in those quick examples, then you can be sure that you can hear and see Jesus when you ask for Him.

We know that He will show up when you do because He wants to connect with you even more than you want to communicate with Him. God answers yes to heart desires that are in alignment with His will. This means that when you agree to meet with God, He shows up and moves to align you according to His will.

If at first you don't see Him in 3D vivid color, that's perfectly OK. You can be grateful with glimpses, sounds, smells, pictures, feelings, or single words initially. Don't allow your expectations to rob you of blessings by dismissing the small beginnings. It will get easier with practice. The more you dialogue journal, the more you will be able to see and hear God.

Hopefully, by the end of this book experience, you and Jesus will be intimate friends and you will be seeing and hearing from Him like a pro. Give yourself some learning curve time. Practice makes perfect. You will meet Jesus in your special place and then He will take the scene where it needs to go.

Encounter Jesus: Your Special Place

Have your notebook or journal handy to record your experience. For many of the encounters in this book series, there will be guided imagery links where you can listen to my voice as a guide. Not every encounter will need this as you get more experienced with your special place. All guided imageries and lyric video links can be found on my website www.PattySadallah.com/Experience-Jesus/ Keep this page open as you read through the book so those links are handy. They are easily identified by book page number and title.

Special Place Encounter http://bit.ly/2g8v8iu.

You can experience this first *special place* encounter by clicking this link. Just relax and listen as I walk you through your first Jesus encounter. Make sure you record what you see and hear Jesus doing with you.

If you do not have a computer, find someone who will talk through these steps for you. It would be too difficult to keep your eyes on Jesus and keep track of these steps as you go. Make sure you keep the experience going long past when the audio instruction has finished. Don't jam the receiver on God just because the audio instruction is complete.

Here are the steps to this encountering experience of meeting Jesus in your special place: Get in a comfortable position where you will not be disturbed. Relax.

- For best results, spend time worshipping and praising Him even before you open in prayer to welcome His presence.

- Begin with a prayer that welcomes God and invites Him to come to speak to you today. You are only wanting to speak to Jesus. Let Him know that He is who you desire to meet today.

- Let God show you a beautiful place. It could be somewhere you have been before that brings you comfort, or it could be a paradise-like place from your imagination. He knows the place, so just relax.

- With the eyes of your heart, take your time to look carefully on the screen of your mind to the left, to the right, directly in front of you, up above your head, and then down.

- Take in all that you can see, hear, and smell in this place. Awaken all your senses. But don't judge or try harder regarding how much you can see at first.

- After getting a picture in your mind of this place, turn around and see Jesus walking toward you. Don't strain with the eyes of your heart, just relax and allow yourself to see and sense what you can.

- See Jesus come up to you and give you a big loving hug. Feel His embrace. Soak in the feeling of His Presence.

- Sit, lay down or begin walking with Jesus. Ask Him a question. These questions will change as you work through this book. Your first question is: How do you feel about me, LORD? Tune to flowing pictures, thoughts, and emotions, as these are coming from the Spirit within (Jn. 7:37-39).

- Allow Jesus to completely take over the scene. Watch, listen and feel what He is doing.

- Write down what you see Him doing, saying, and showing you. Don't question it, just write it down in simple child-like faith.

- Feel free to ask Him another question. Keep the conversation going like you would with a dear friend. The more you do, the more He will show you.

- Let Jesus keep speaking and showing you what He wants until you feel like the conversation has ended.

Give thanks for whatever you got from Jesus. It may be that you could only get a feeling, a small picture, or one word. Anything you receive is a good start.

If you haven't been recording the experience as it is happening, write it down now. Thank God for what He showed you. Consult Appendix A for more tips on Hearing God's voice. You will get more skilled at this as you work through the book.

Each time you encounter God, ask for Him to give you more. If you are seeing pictures, ask Him to explain what they mean. If you hear Him clearly, ask Him for more visions. Remember to thank Him no matter what He gives you!

In the Hands of the Potter by Casting Crowns

https://bit.ly/33wD3eI

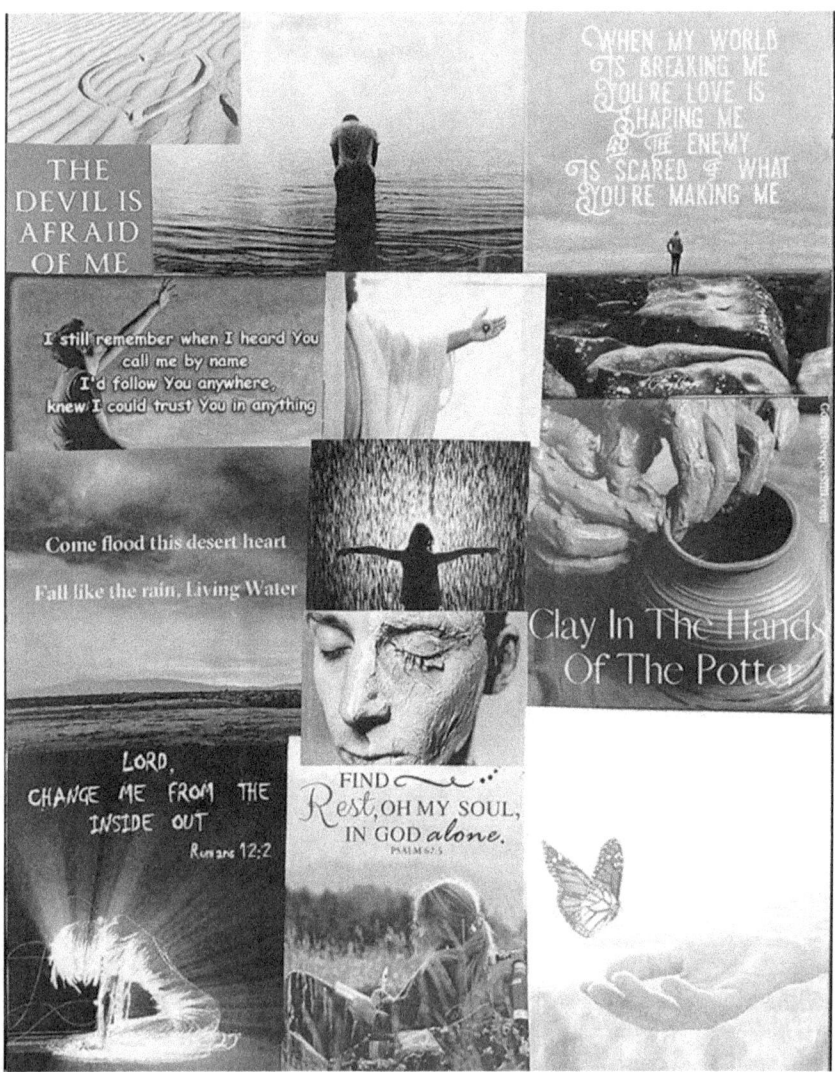

Encountering the
DIRECTION of God
Introduction

⌒⫘⌒

One day at church, my Pastor was preaching on the Potter and the Clay. He spoke for a short while and then a potter sculpted a pot as we worshiped for about three songs. The Lord showed me some interesting truths as I watched this skillful artist turn this lump of clay into a beautiful vessel before my eyes.

> Isaiah 64:8 Yet, O LORD, You are our Father; We are the clay, and You are the Potter, And we all are the work of Your hand.

God doesn't just want to save you. He wants to mold you into the very best version of yourself. He is the Potter, and you are the clay.

The First thing that struck me was the sponge of water. The Potter was constantly hydrating the clay with water, gently dipping a sponge from the water source and squeezing drops of water all over the clay.

Jesus said,

This is the Living Water that keeps your heart moldable in My hands. Drink deeply of the Living Water every day, or you will get dry, and hard-hearted. Clay needs to be soft in My hands to be moldable.

The potter wrapped his hands around the *l*ump of clay and pulled it up onto a tower-like cylinder and then made a fist and gently pushed it down into the top center creating the opening of the container. While one hand was on the outside of the spinning clay, the other was working on the inside of the vessel. I couldn't see what his hand was doing, but the shape changed from a cylinder to a rounder pot. The movements of the potter's hands were gentle and almost imperceptible, but changes were being made to this pot before my eyes.

I imagined for a second what it must feel like to be the clay, spinning constantly. Without the hands of the potter, the clay could fly off the base and would remain only a useless lump of clay. The clay was nothing apart from the potter. When your life feels like it's spinning out of control, it helps to remember that the Heavenly Potter, Creator God, has you in His gentle and capable hands.

Psalm 139:13-16 (MSG)

Oh yes, you shaped me first inside, then out;
  you formed me in my mother's womb.
I thank you, High God—you're breathtaking!
  Body and soul, I am marvelously made!
  I worship in adoration—what a creation!
You know me inside and out,
  you know every bone in my body;
You know exactly how I was made, bit by bit,
  how I was sculpted from nothing into something.
Like an open book, you watched me grow from conception
to birth;
  all the stages of my life were spread out before you,

The days of my life all prepared
before I'd even lived one day.

Check out this short video of a potter from India making a beautiful pot in less than two minutes.[9]

Making an Earthen Pot
https://youtu.be/Y5rMI6mQ1_k

The potter uses tools to make each pot unique. They gently peel off the parts of clay that are not wanted. Like pruning a tree, God uses your life circumstances and challenges to strengthen you and allow you to grow into who He created you to become.

Every pot has a unique purpose. God perfectly makes each one of us for our purpose. But you must allow Him to mold you. Be pliable in the Father's hands and know that He can always begin again.

Jeremiah 18:1-4

[1] The LORD gave another message to Jeremiah. He said, [2]"Go down to the potter's shop, and I will speak to you there." [3] I

---

[9] Making and Earthen Pot-Pottery from Wild Films India https://youtu.be/Y5rMI6mQ1_k

did as he told me and found the potter working at his wheel. [4]But the jar he was making did not turn out as he had hoped, so he crushed it into a lump of clay again and started over.

[5]Then the LORD gave me this message: [6]"O Israel, can I not do to you as this potter has done to his clay? As the clay is in the potter's hand, so are you in my hand. [7]If I announce that a certain nation or kingdom is to be uprooted, torn down, and destroyed, [8]but then that nation renounces its evil ways, I will not destroy it as I had planned. [9]And if I announce that I will plant and build up a certain nation or kingdom, 10but then that nation turns to evil and refuses to obey me, I will not bless it as I said I would.

The clay cannot mold itself. It needs to be molded by an outside force. The pliability of clay is related to the level of water. Without water, it becomes dry and hard. Thirst is a need that must be satisfied, or you die. God causes you to thirst for Him and the living water satisfies your soul.

I noticed that one of the potter's hands was always on the outside of the spinning pot while his other hand was making changes that I could not see. This represents how God changes us first on the inside and then on the outside. Those imperceptible changes shaped the pot for its purpose. We can't always see what the Potter is doing when He's shaping us from the inside out.

On the journey to discovering the direction of God, you must learn who you were created to be first. When you become who God needs you to be, then, He can prepare and position you for what He needs you to do. Alignment with God's will and intention for you is necessary to live out that destined purpose. You must learn that you can do nothing of any significant value apart from God.

What would happen if the Potter took his hand off the wheel? The clay would wobble and fly off the wheel. That's what your life looks like when you face challenges and take your eyes off God. Your life spins out of control.

God's loving discipline can feel like you are being crushed. But it is so He can create you into a better version of yourself. You can become the person more capable and suited for who He called you to be and what He called you to do.

Skipping Stones

Jesus and I were standing on the shore of the Sea of Galilee when He handed me a small translucent stone of light. It was warm in my hand and it had a holographic nature, for when I moved it, I could see changing words that were there and then not there: love, peace, joy. These are the Fruit of the Spirit words; they are God's character, His glory in the stone.

The stone was warm, a comforting kind of warm like a blanket right out of the dryer and wrapped around you on a cold and dreary fall day. Comforting like the Comforter. It felt good in my hand. Then Jesus told me to fling it into the sea like one would a skipping stone. I didn't want to throw it away because it felt precious to me, but I would, because the Lord wanted me to.

I held the stone between my thumb and middle finger rubbing the warm smooth surface and then flicked it with my wrist. It flew and landed on top of the water. Unexpectedly, as soon as it hit the surface, it multiplied to five stones, not dropping into the water but still lit up on the water's surface. Each stone created ring ripples all at once. Then the five stones multiplied again and repeated the pattern of multiplying, skipping, creating rings, multiplying, skipping, and creating rings until the lights and the ripples filled the whole sea as far as my eye could see.

I was struck by the beauty and the power of it. I turned to Jesus and I asked him what it meant. Jesus answered,

> *"This is the multiplying effect of people finding Me and being changed by My love. The stones represent people moved so much by My love that they contagiously share it in their own unique ways, just as I've created them to do. Your calling is to show people the way to that love."*

God is a God of multiplication.

I hadn't noticed it because I was distracted by the beauty, but then I realized I had another stone in my hand. Jesus said,

> *"Every stone is an opportunity, a new encounter, an intervention to help people find my love. Abide in Me and listen to My voice for these are opportunities to throw the next stone and start the beauty all over again."*

Then the Lord led me to...

> 2 Thessalonians 1:11 [11] With this in view, we constantly pray for you, that our God will count you worthy of your calling [to faith] and with [His] power fulfill every desire for goodness, and complete [your] every work of faith,

Thank you that you are a God of multiplication and that your love spreads to the multitudes. Thank you, Lord, that you trust me with the priceless stone of your Truth. Equip me, Lord, to be a good steward of this precious treasure. In Jesus' Name, Amen.

Lessons from My Calling Project

When I was taking Biblical Research Methods for my doctorate, my assignment was to research something connected to my calling. Initially, when I began the search for the topic, the Lord gave me just the word; "love". Love is such a big word. God is love and the entire Bible is one big love story, so this topic category was a bit overwhelming for me. I consulted the Lord through journaling and this is what He said,

> *I want you to know the meaning of the love I wrote to you about in the love letter I gave you when you were saved. Look at it again. Follow the trail that it takes you. I speak of everlasting love. Look at this letter and the key aspects of love that are in it. They are the ones I want you to explore. Make this a personal journey into My love. When you learn more about My love, you will be more able to love.*
>
> *Your journey begins as it did for you in 1979 – with that love letter. It will show you the way! I AM God; believe it and be satisfied!*

That was exactly what I needed! The bold words are those that were biblically researched for the project. The letter again is here:

> *Everyone longs to give themselves **completely** to someone – to have a **deep soul relationship** with another, to be **loved thoroughly** and **exclusively**. But God, to a Christian says,*
>
> *No, not until you are **satisfied** and **fulfilled** and **content** with being **loved** by Me alone. I **love** you, my child, and until you **discover** that only in Me is your **satisfaction** to be found, you will not be capable of the perfect human relationship that I have planned for you. You'll never be **united** with another until you are **united** with Me – **exclusive** of anyone or anything else, **exclusive** of any other desires or longings. I want you to stop planning, stop wishing, and allow Me to give you the most **thrilling plan** existing – one that you can't imagine. I want you to have the **best**. Please **allow** Me to bring it to you. Just keep **experiencing** that **satisfaction** of **knowing** that **I AM**. Keep **learning** and **listening** to the things I tell you... You must wait.*

*Don't be anxious. Don't worry. Don't **look** around at the things others have gotten or that I've given to them. Don't **look** at the things you think you want. You just keep **looking** off and away up to Me, or you'll miss what I want to show you.*

*Then, when you're **ready**, I'll surprise you with the **love** far more wonderful than any would ever dream of. You see, until you are **ready** and until the one I have for you is **ready**, I'm working even this very minute to have both of you **ready** at the same time. Until you are both **satisfied exclusively** with me and with the life I have **prepared** for you, you won't be able to **experience** the **love** that exemplifies your relationship with Me... And this is the **perfect love**.*

*And dear one, I want you to have this most wonderful **love**, I want you to see in the flesh a picture of your **relationship** with Me, and enjoy materially and concretely the **everlasting union** of beauty and **perfection** and love that I offer you with myself.*

***Know** that I **love** you **utterly, I AM** God. **Believe** it and be **satisfied**."*

Life Application Takeaways

When I received that love letter in 1979, I had only been a believer for a couple of days. When I read it, I felt comfort believing that it was a promise from the Lord that He would bring me a future husband. At that time in my spiritual development, it was a letter about helping a heartbroken girl in this world.

When the Lord gave that letter back to me in 2012 when I was writing *Clips that Move Mountains*, I could see that the "true love" was not a human, but God Himself, and saw it as a message about the need for an intimate relationship with Him. I still didn't see the connection between His love and my calling then.

After this Biblical research assignment, I can see more layers of meaning in that love letter. Now I can see that being satisfied, fulfilled and content in this life is directly connected to how close my relationship is with God. The more I encounter the Lord personally, the more I can see, feel and think like Him. The more his love is real to me. The letter shows me that God is ALL and is in ALL. But this is not just for me. This applies to you too!

You can't love anyone properly or at all aside from God. Love comes from God and flows to you and then out to others. If you want to have any type of "perfect human relationship," it will come only with the surrender, humility, and faith that comes from conforming your heart to God's. This is His transformational way.

God created you to desire to be loved thoroughly and exclusively. Apart from God, it is impossible to be loved the way He created you to desire to be loved. So you need to find your way back to the Author of love. God wants to be your one true love. "Exclusive of anything or anyone else." He is saying that He wants you to lay down all of the idols in your heart and fix your eyes on Jesus alone. The more you are with Him, the more you will become like Him, and the more useful you will be to the kingdom.

He wants you to "stop planning, stop wishing." Planning and wishing imply that you are in the driver's seat. That is striving instead of trusting and resting. That's what it looks like to be swimming against the wind and the waves. He wants you to listen, wait and only act when you feel compelled to by His compassionate love. He wants you to trust Him with your life. When you do, He will begin to reveal the thrilling plan that He has for you. And He will prepare you for the work He has for you. His plan will be greater than you could ever imagine for yourself, because if you could do it with your own strength, then it's too small and not from God.

He will give you a glimpse of your future, as a promise of the fruit of the calling if you will stay the course. He is preparing you for that future even as you read this book. The good plans promised to every believer in Jeremiah 29:11 are God's best plans. He wants you to have the best!

You need to cooperate with Him to have this fruitful future. He says, "Please allow me to bring it to you." You must partner with the Lord with these plans. If you take your eyes off Him, you could forfeit this future. You need to make sure that you don't get in your way and disallow the Holy Spirit from doing His job.

God clarifies that satisfaction comes from knowing that "I AM." This kind of knowledge is of the most personal type. He wants you to have the satisfaction of His very presence in your life. Here The faith you need comes from trusting Him. You trust people that you know, like, and have found believable and trustworthy. This trust can only grow with time and a relationship with God.

He prepared you by teaching you to keep your eyes on Him at all times, so you don't miss what He is doing or go off on bunny trails of distraction. Stay the course! The Lord doesn't want you to look at the world or the fruit of other people. He doesn't want anything to take your eyes off Him.

And then, when He decides you are ready, He will surprise you with the perfect love. This is the combination of the intimate love relationship with Him and the compassion-motivated calling that He has for you. The impact that awaits you in your life is the fruit of your thrilling plan.

> This book is the guide to your journey. It is my calling to
> show people the way to God's love. Say "yes" and "amen" to

God because He said: ***Know*** *that I* ***love*** *you* ***utterly, I AM God. Believe*** *it and be* ***satisfied.***"

What the Lord had to say...

Lord, help me understand more about the connection between your compassion and callings. What does the love letter have to do with my life's purpose?

> *Love is what everything I do is all about. So it's what you and all believers are about. I've created you to show people the way, to help them tap into their own plans and purposes I have for them. Remember, to be a guide, you need to become an expert in the terrain.*

> *The love letter shows the benefit, the outcome of the perfect love connection between Me and you: Me and any believer. Your job is to learn the terrain of helping people sense Me, My heart, and grow close enough to Me to trust Me with their lives and plans. You can't do that until it becomes second nature for you. Learning this lesson is your job now in the wilderness.*

> *Most people think inaccurately about what a calling is. People think that they are serving according to their calling if they serve the Lord in areas of their personal passion that is, their selfish motivation. This kind of service is without the anointing and power of the Holy Spirit. They inaccurately feel as though I will come alongside them because their motivation is to serve Me. This mindset leads to burnout, frustration, and a sense of martyr pride. It comes from striving and not resting.*

> *The key difference here is they have a "what" focus and not a "why" focus. They think that what they do is the key. People especially in the Western culture get wrapped up in their identities based on what they do for a living. This is not important to Me. The important thing is "why," which is the motivational heart of God to reach the lost and hurting*

people and "who" they are becoming. To find your calling, you need to find your God! When you connect My Heart to your heart, I will move you accordingly.

Lord, speak to me about the love letter as it relates to this Truth.

"People get caught up in this world as if this is the only world. This world was created only for the next world, heaven. Your challenge is to help people understand their plans. Their way to the Father. The letter speaks of the "thrilling plan" and the One True Love. People cannot have satisfaction in this life until they find satisfaction in Me. They can't love others properly and do what they are gifted to do, without My anointing power. Satisfaction in this life is wrapped up in learning that it's not about this life at all. It's about Me."

"The love, the power, and the direction all come from clearly seeing how you fit into My big plan like a puzzle piece in the big overall plan. Help them find the Way, the flow, the ocean waves, and the wind in their sails that carry them to their niche. Then you have fulfilled your calling and found your way. Faith, hope, trust, love, and all the other love characteristics you are discovering along the way are the bread crumbs to follow when finding the way."

The Names you will Meet

- When you meet the **Truth,** you will discover the Biblical promises to anchor your faith and how to trust in those promises for your life and future. Learning how to trust in the Truth allows you to align yourself with who God created you to be. This is the first key step in your discovery of your direction and purpose. The key lessons on this Name are related to *understanding your Christ Identity and aligning with God's purposes.*

- When you meet the **Good Shepherd,** you will learn how God perfectly guides, cares and protects you. Surrendering your will to that of the Good Shepherd begins to align you with His plans for you. Cooperating with God's plans leads to living a life of grace and fruit-bearing by your Christ identity. The key lesson with this Name is to learn *how to follow Him so that you remain under His perfect care and protection.*

- *The **Author of your Story** has an ideal life for you. There are clues from your life about how God created you uniquely with certain interests and abilities. And the lessons of your life have prepared you for your destiny. How do you share the story with others as your reflection of the gospel? How has God written your story up to this point and where is he going with it? *Learning how to cooperate for this best plan and how to abide in His presence are key lessons of this Name.*

- The **Waymaker** will show you how you fit into the kingdom plan along with others in the body of Christ. You will get in touch with your unique gifts and see how He has been setting the table for your future and Kingdom impact behind the scenes. How can you pay attention while He's working everything out to your good? *The key lesson is how to understand how to properly prepare for your destiny and fit in unity with the body of Christ.*

- When you meet the **Supernatural Provider,** you will learn that what God calls, He perfectly equips. His provision is not limited to natural resources but includes the power of the indwelling Holy Spirit. Learn how to steward the powerful manifestation gifts of the Holy Spirit and be increasingly trusted with them for greater impact.

Experience Jesus for your Direction

- Prepare your heart for your encounter with God by finding a comfortable place where you will not be disturbed.

- Breathe deeply and relax.

- Then visualize yourself as a child and go to your special place.

- Meet Jesus there and play with Him for a few minutes.

- Jesus will show you or speak to you about the journey He is taking you on to discover your direction.

- Ask Him for a glimpse of your fruit-bearing destiny. See what you are doing and for whom you are serving.

- Then, Jesus will talk with you about what would need to happen for you to cooperate with this future. What does He want to specifically work on with you to make you ready for that future?

- Make sure you ask Him all the questions you need to be clear, so you know what to focus on when you go through the rest of this book.

- Take all the time you need and record it all in your journal.

Jesus I Believe by Big Daddy Weave

https://bit.ly/36dCTM1

Meet the Truth

As you begin your journey to discover the direction of God, it's important to anchor yourself in the Truth of who God is and who you are in Him. Let's begin by understanding the rules of your body, soul, and spirit.

Body, Soul & Spirit

Your physical body was created for this natural world, and it only exists while you're alive on earth. It's natural for us to feel the most connected to our bodies and to focus on the realities of this natural realm. But it is limiting to think of yourself as only your body.

Your soul is the part of you that contains your mind, will, and emotions. When you die, your soul is the part of you that goes to its eternal destination. So, your soul lives first on earth, then in. heaven. This is why the Bible talks about saving souls.

> Matthew 10:28 Do not be afraid of those who kill the body but cannot kill the soul.

God can move you along the path of spiritual maturity when you know how your mind, will, and emotions cause you to make decisions that affect your relationships and life.

Your spirit is the part of you that God created specifically to connect with Him. Connecting with God helps you merge with His mind, will, and emotions. Everyone has been given the eyes and ears of their hearts to be able to communicate with the Lord. And when you accept Jesus as your Lord and Savior, the Holy Spirit makes Himself at home in your heart.

This is what I heard the Lord had to say to help us understand the body, soul, and spirit relationally.

> *The goal is to realize that your spirit is the part of you that abides in Me. You can turn to Me for supernatural Truths and capabilities at all times. True victory in life comes when you know how to live out of that Truth 24/7.*
>
> *True fruit-bearing Christians have found the way to live out of the spirit while living in the body and addressing the needs of their soul. This can only come from trusting the Truth and believing that the Truth is for YOU.*

100 Verses on Truth

To understand the Truth, here is a site with 100 verses related to Truth.[10] https://www.openbible.info/topics/word_of_Truth.

I meditated on them and sorted them by the categories: *what Truth is not, what Truth is, what Truth does, so we can, so He can.* I highly recommend that you meditate on this list of verses yourself as there's a lot of depth here. But I will summarize categorically what I learned from this exercise.

---

[10] https://www.openbible.info/topics/word_of_Truth

What Truth is Not

Truth is not a thing to know but a Person to know. Jesus is the Truth.

> John 14:6 Jesus said to him, "[a]I am the [only] Way [to God] and the [real] Truth and the [real] Life; no one comes to the Father but through Me.

Since the Truth is Jesus, it makes sense that you can't find Truth in worldly knowledge. It is not changeable or fashionable. It does not conform with cultural trends. Jesus is not selfish or loveless, so everything true will be consistent with His character and nature. Jesus explains this Himself as He challenged the Pharisees who misunderstood the truth.

> John 8:42-44 [42] Jesus said to them, "If God were your Father [but He is not], you would love *and* recognize Me, for I came from God [out of His very presence] and have arrived *here*. For I have not even come on My own initiative [as self-appointed], but He [is the One who] sent Me. [43] Why do you misunderstand what I am saying? It is because [your spiritual ears are deaf and] you are unable to hear [the truth of] My word. [44] You are of *your* father the devil, and it is your will to practice the desires [which are characteristic] of your father. He was a murderer from the beginning and does not stand in the truth because there is no truth in him. When he lies, he speaks what is natural to him, for he is a liar and the father of lies *and* half-truths.

What Truth Is

Jesus is also known as the Word. Every word in the Bible was God-breathed and is true.

> 2 Timothy 3:16 All Scripture is God-breathed [given by divine inspiration] and is profitable for instruction, for conviction [of sin], for correction [of error and restoration to obedience], for training in righteousness [learning to live in conformity to God's will, both publicly and privately—behaving honorably with personal integrity and moral courage];

The Word is perfectly righteous, endures forever, is motivated by love, and is unchanging. Every word in the Bible is intentional, has a clear purpose, and is energized by God's empowering presence. Understanding the truth for your life is tied to His Kingdom's purpose and your role in it.

> John 16:13 But when He, the Spirit of Truth, comes, He will guide you into all the truth [full and complete truth]. For He will not speak on His own initiative, but He will speak whatever He hears [from the Father—the message regarding the Son], and He will disclose to you what is to come [in the future].

What Truth Does

The Truth prepares, empowers, and equips you to be transformed into your Christ identity. God reveals His mind, will, and emotion which increases your wisdom and discernment. Your cooperation with His Truth aligns you with God and powerfully sets you free from bondage. The Truth shows you the way to salvation and gives you the tools and the guidance to partner with Him for your fruit-bearing destiny.

The Truth of your Identity

I found a wonderful resource by Reasons for Hope Jesus that listed 101 verses related to the truth of your identity in Christ.[11]

---

[11] Reasons for Hope the Truth of your Identity in Christ Resource. https://reasonsforhopejesus.com/wp-content/uploads/2018/03/Identity_In_Christ.pdf

This resource has broken scripture references into categories. There are 66 "I am," 33 "I have", and five "I know" statements backed up by scripture. Each statement summarizes a referenced truth from the Word. I highly recommend that you print this resource and meditate on these 101 Truths as God directs. Look at these statements as a road map to aligning with your Christ-Identity. Doing so moves you toward leading your best fruit-bearing life.

Here are some examples of these statements and their scripture references:

- I am set free by the truth (John 8:31-33)

- I am freed from the power of sin (1 Peter 2:24)

- I am protected by the power of His name (John 1711)

- I am conformed to the image of Christ (Romans 8:29)

- I am blessed with every spiritual blessing (Ephesians 1:3)

- I am God's handiwork, created in Christ Jesus to do good works (Ephesians 2:10)

- I am led by the spirit of God (Romans 8:14)

- I have the spirit of wisdom and revelation in His knowledge (Ephesians 1:17)

- I have peace with God through Jesus (Romans 5:1)

- I have the whole armor of God and stand firm (Ephesians 6:13)

- I have fellowship with Jesus Christ (1 Corinthians 1:9)

- I know the hope of my calling (Ephesians 1:18)

- I know the riches of His inheritance in the saints (Ephesians 1:18)
- I know the exceeding greatness of His power to me. (Ephesians 119)

So You Can

The Truth allows you to transform into the best version of yourself-your Christ Identity. When you are set free from the bondage of self, you align with God's perfect will and rightly agree with His best for you. This is where fulfillment and satisfaction are found. Knowing God intimately leads to bearing fruit in unity with the body of Christ. You are safe under His protective umbrella when you make godly choices and bring heaven down to earth.

Staying in tune with God's Truth allows you to follow God properly. He lovingly shows you when you have gone off track. And when you see yourself rightly, you can confess and repent and realign yourself with His good purposes. This is how you become light in a dark world for those for whom he would have us to influence. Your Christ-Identity brings God's love into every circumstance.

Encountering God as you have learned to do in this book series, by the specific Names of God, allows you to relationally understand the Truth. You're not trying to understand the Word of God in your head, but from the author of the Word directly.

The Chronicles of Narnia is a fantasy series of books by C.S. Lewis that has been adapted to radio, TV, stage, and film. The book series spans the beginning of the creation of Narnia to its end. Aslan, the Lion represents Jesus and was likely inspired by the Name of God ' the Lion of the Tribe of Judah'.

In this scene from the final book and film *The Voyage of the Dawn Treader,* we see the children saying goodbye to Narnia.

Know Me Here: Narnia Clip[12]
https://youtu.be/Rw7zG4EQ7rU

When Lucy asks Aslan if they will see Him again, he says they will recognize him by another name. But that their experiences in Narnia will help them recognize him there.

This is true of your encountering experiences with this book series as well. When you have encounters with God as His unique names, you build memories of personal times with Him and begin to see Jesus as the Truth. There is no better way to internalize the Truth than to personalize Him. This is why God created a way for you to encounter Him.

Why we Struggle to Believe: The Trust Factor

Without emotional intimacy, there is no real connection with God. For many, it's easy to believe God's truth for somebody else, but they

---

[12] Film clip from The Chronicles of Narnia - The Voyage of the Dawn Treader Final Goodbyes https://youtu.be/Rw7zG4EQ7rU

struggle to believe it for themselves. This is what Jesus spoke to me about that:

> *Truth is Truth, regardless of you! You are not a factor in Truth itself. Truth is not dependent on your influence. Just like you are not a condition of whether fire burns. It burns because I created it to burn. You cannot will yourself to live without oxygen. Gravity will cause you to fall off a cliff. These are all examples of truths that exist apart from your influence.*
>
> *Trusting the Truth is a factor that will affect your life. At a young age, you learn to trust that fire burns, that you need oxygen and that falling from high places will hurt you. Your trust in those truths influences how you think and behave as a result.*
>
> *Trust is demonstrated by respecting and honoring those truths and the boundaries that keep you safe related to them. There are consequences to disrespecting those truths, just like there is with gravity and fire. Understanding their blessings and their rules influence your behavior.*
>
> *Your personal understanding of Me as the Truth is enhanced tremendously by experiencing Me personally. The more you encounter Me directly, the more you will realize that I am a Promise Keeper and that every Word I promised in the Bible is True and for you. I AM here and always accessible. I share My heart with you and fully equip you for your purpose and calling. I turn every challenge, trial, and even tragedy in your life for your good when you seek Me for the lessons I have for you to learn by them.*

The scripture at the bottom of my journal where He said this was:

Psalm 111:10 (NIV) The fear of the Lord is the beginning of wisdom; all who follow His precepts have a good understanding. To Him belongs eternal praise.

Trusting Leads to Believing Him

Who do you trust? Typically, it's people with whom you feel safe, loved, and have been able to count on in times of need.

If you struggle with trust in your life, you will have trouble trusting God. Below are some reasons why you may struggle with trust in general. As you read through these possible trust issues, be honest with yourself about which ones may be true for you.

Past hurts can lead you to protect yourself by holding trust back grudgingly. Rather than trusting someone until they prove untrustworthy, you may not trust them until they prove themselves trustworthy.

Hurt people hurt people. Past heartbreaks and wounds can be weaponized if they are not healed by the Lord. To protect your heart, you distance people. If this is your tendency, then your heart posture is to assume that the Lord will hurt or disappoint you and you will choose to distance yourself from Him as well. Many people interpret behavior as untrustworthy by assuming negative heart motivations that are not there. This misassumption pushes people away.

> 1 Corinthians 4:5 So do not go on passing judgment before the appointed time, but wait until the Lord comes, for He will both bring to light the [secret] things that are hidden in darkness and disclose the motives of the hearts. Then each one's praise will come from God.

Maybe you are afraid of giving up control. You feel that giving up control will lead to heartbreak, so you withhold trust. The lie in play is that safety is defined by what you can control. Control is a myth. The very safest place you can ever be is inside God's will.

Perhaps you suffer from unrealistic expectations. I remember hearing once that all anger and disappointments can be traced to unmet expectations. When you hold in your mind that a thing has to go exactly as you expect, you will be disappointed. The enemy loves to whisper in your ear that it was God that disappointed you. Believing this lie makes God smaller in your mind. God's ways are higher and wiser than your ways and His timing is always perfect. He is the Omni-God.

All these tendencies reveal trust in the world or your understanding, rather than trusting the Truth of who God is and your spiritual identity.

Come to your Senses

In the story of the prodigal son detailed in Luke 15:11-32, we are introduced to a man with two sons. The younger son asked his father for his inheritance so that he could travel to distant lands and live recklessly. The other son stayed dutifully behind and served his father.

After completely wasting his father's fortune, the younger son, found himself sitting in a pigpen penniless and hungry.

> Luke 15:17 [17] But when he [finally] **came to his senses**, he said, 'How many of my father's hired men have more than enough food, while I am dying here of hunger!

The Hebrew word for 'come to one's senses' is *ananéphó*. It means to return to soberness, come to yourself, to become sober again, recover sound sense. It means to be set free from the snare of the devil and to return to a sound mind. It is the awakening of the moral guideline of knowing right from wrong from God's perspective.

This spiritual awakening is necessary for you to move from the limiting lies that keep you from trusting God, to the truth that will set you free from them. Your thoughts and behaviors can cause you to think that you are disqualified from the blessings of the Truth. Do not let your mouth confess such lies. Do you agree with bondages, or do you agree with the Truth?

Coming to your senses is agreeing with the Truth of who you are and what God has promised you, regardless of behaviors. You are not the total of your mistakes or failures. The Blood of Jesus qualified you. Ask God to show you the Truth. Then be willing to agree with Him.

The very best way to trust anyone is to spend time with them and realize that you are safe in their presence. God is trustworthy, and time spent with Him will prove that to you. In our encounter exercises for this Name, the Lord will begin the work needed to break down those barriers and create pathways for you to trust Him for His promises.

So He Can

God created you so you can be part of His story. There is a purpose for you to fulfill as part of the overall Kingdom plan. God desires to work with and through you and it brings Him great joy to live with you in Truth.

God desires to show you the way to your most fulfilling life here on earth and in heaven. Pam, one of my Spirit Life Circle mentors led a group of us through a guided encounter with Jesus. The experience had us take a journey.

The journey began on a dusty dirt path. We were to pay attention to how the dirt clouded up for each step. Then the road was made of small pebbles. We approached a fork in the road and needed to make a choice: Do we go to the left or the right? We made our choices.

The journey progressed and as it did the pebbles became bigger stones until they become boulders blocking the road. Then she had us look for Jesus and ask Him questions about the journey. Some focused on the fork in the road and asked about what would've happened if they made the other choice. Others focused on the rocks and the increased difficulty of the journey.

I had seen Jesus with me for the entire journey, while some others needed to look for Him when things got difficult. We were to ask him the question in our hearts about this trek.

Lord, what do you want to say to me about the rocky and slippery path?

Nothing of any value comes without stretching and challenges. These are necessary to make you stronger. I am always with you. You are never alone. When you fall, I reach out and grab your hand to steady you. You are always safe with Me.

Lord, what are some rocky times right ahead of me?

This is an important Kingdom season. I need you to rise up and be the head and not the tail. I will increase your platform of influence. As a result, there will be a religious spirit that will come against you. Reach for my hand. And remember, they persecuted Me too. In fact, they persecute Me when they persecute you. This is true of all my chosen Spirit-led warriors and workers.

Don't take the challenges personally. Hold my hand as I steady you and keep on walking. The road will get steeper and more challenging. But oh the view from the top is so worth it!

I love you, My dear child. You bring me great joy. We will do amazing things together!

Thank you, Lord! I love you too. Thank you for being with me every step of the way!

Do you really Trust Me?

I wanted to share my experience of the "Stretch your Trust Limits" encounter that the Lord gave me when I was writing this chapter. The exercise leads to the Lord revealing an area that you need to work on concerning your trust in Him.

The Lord reminded me of a film clip from *Despicable Me and the Plot to Steal the Moon* movie. I had recently seen this section of the movie while babysitting my grandkids only days before. I could not find an appropriately cut clip of this film scene but in the movie, former villain Gru had his heart softened by three young orphans. He was trying to save them from an arch-nemesis villain Vector who had kidnapped them.

Gru was standing on the wing of an airplane and the three children were in a spaceship-like aircraft. Gru told the girls to jump, and he would catch them. The two little ones jumped and he caught them and the oldest was grabbed by Vector before she could jump. Gru saved all the kids in the end.

The Lord reminded me of this scene, and I was suddenly the one on the spaceship seeing Jesus on the wing of the plane. He said,

Jump. I promise to catch you.

It's you, Lord. I trust You because You promised. And I jumped and He caught me. But a moment later, I was on the spaceship again and my husband was on the wing of the plane. I heard Jesus' voice say,

Jump. I promise to catch you.

I hesitated. It was easy to trust Him. He's the Omni-God after all. But now He's asking me to trust George. I was afraid.

It was still My promise. I am in George too, you know. If I promise he will catch you, you need to trust Me that I can keep that promise, even thru other people.

I'm asking people to trust that what you are teaching is from Me. It lines up with Biblical principles. I need you to trust that I am in control, and I work powerful and miraculous things through people all the time.

Do you trust Me?

Yes. I do Lord. I will picture George as being covered by You and I will jump. So, I looked to see Jesus' covering over George and I jumped. He caught me.

God is God, even when He is working through imperfect human beings. He can work through you too!

Encountering the Truth:
Stretch your Trust Limits (link)

Steps to this encounter

The goal of this encounter is to have the Lord help you understand an area for which you have struggled to trust Him and address it together.

- Meet Jesus in your special place and play with Him for a while simply enjoying His presence.

- The Lord will take you on an adventure that will stretch your trust limits.

- Pay attention to what He is showing you. Everything that you remember is significant.

- Capture the entire experience and make sure you ask Him as many questions as you need to be able to understand what He's trying to show you.

- Then ask Him what step you can take today to move in the direction of greater trust in Him.

- Make sure that you thank Him for what He showed you and that you obey that step.

Staring Contest (link)

Steps to this encounter

To aid in this encounter, begin by finding a picture of Jesus that you can look at for a while. I particularly like the Prince of Peace drawing of Jesus by Akiane.

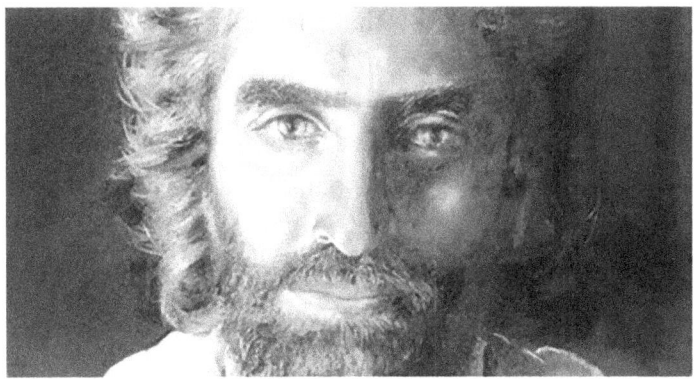

- Meet Jesus and special place as a child.

- He and you will find a place to sit, cross-legged and Face-to-face.

- Hold hands and look directly into each other's eyes.

- Try not to blink. Look into His eyes without looking away.

- Write down your experience including how it made you feel and what you learned about Him and yourself in the staring contest.

Share a Secret (link)

Steps to this encounter

Jesus has been with you your entire life. There is no secret that He doesn't know, but in the action of sharing it with Him you will learn that you can trust Him, even in areas you don't feel comfortable trusting anyone else.

- Meet Jesus in your special place and spend some time just playing and enjoying each other.

- You will have a sense of what it is that Jesus wants you to share with Him.

- See yourself whisper this secret in His ear.

- Then, watch how Jesus responds. What does He have to say or show you about this secret? Allow Him to minister to you in any way you need.

- Capture the entire experience in your journal.

I Will Follow by Chris Tomlin

https://youtu.be/-XnPL3LtxpA

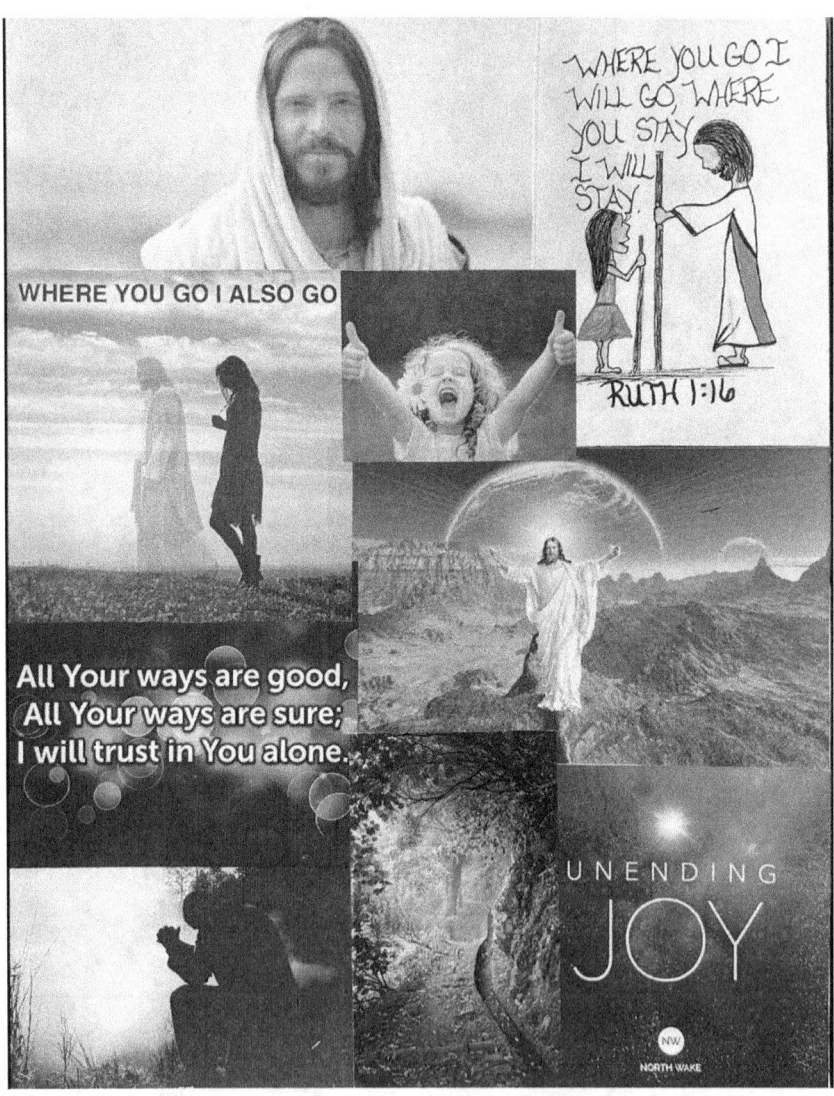

Meet the Good Shepherd

While teaching the parable of the Good Shepherd, Jesus said,

John 10:11 I am the Good Shepherd The Good Shepherd [d] lays down His [own] life for the sheep.

Looking at each of the keywords in this verse, we learn more about why Jesus named Himself this.

- **I AM** is *eimi* the self-existing God who was, is, and always will be.

- **Good** is *kalos* which means beautiful, of noble character, hope, praiseworthy, excellent, goodness, admirable, superior, wholesome, and delightful.

- **Shepherd** is *poimén* which means the feeder, protector, ruler, and caretaker. This is also the same word for pastor which is someone the Lord raises to care for the total well-being of the flock.

- **Lays down** is *tithémi* which means selfless, to set down, lay aside, put in place, establish and ordain.

- **Life** is *psuché* which means vital breath, soul, the self.

Sheep in this context is referring to Jesus' people. The word for sheep simply means sheep, but it was interesting to learn that the origin word for sheep is *probainó* which means to go forward, to advance. Jesus' role as our Good Shepherd is to move us forward by caring, guiding, protecting, and defending us.

The Parable of the Good Shepherd

Let's look at the entire parable of the Good Shepherd in pieces so we can truly understand what this Name means. Jesus told this parable because shepherding was central to the cultural reality at the time. God speaks in your language. That doesn't just mean English, French or German, etc. He speaks in the vernacular of your common experience.

Because shepherding is not something commonly understood by many in our own culture, it helps to give some cultural context to this Name.

> John 10:1-18 "I assure you *and* most solemnly say to you, he who does not enter by the door into the sheepfold, but climbs up from some other place [on the stone wall], that one is a thief and a robber. ² But he who enters by the door is the shepherd of the sheep [the .protector and provider]. ³ The [a]doorkeeper opens [the gate] for this man, and the sheep hear his voice *and* pay attention to it. And [knowing that they listen] he calls his own sheep by name and leads them out [to pasture].

What we learned in these few verses of this parable is that the Good Shepherd in part is another name for the Savior. Jesus is speaking of the exclusive way to salvation. Many other religions try to leap over the fence and believe that they can receive salvation their own way. But Jesus is making it clear that He is the door and the doorkeeper.

> [4] When he has brought all his own *sheep* outside, he walks on ahead of them, and the sheep follow him because they know his voice *and* recognize his call. [5] They will never follow a stranger, but will run away from him, because they do not know the voice of strangers." [6] Jesus used this figure of speech with them, but they did not understand what He was talking about.

> [7] So Jesus said again, "I assure you *and* most solemnly say to you, I am [b]the Door for the sheep [leading to life]. [8] All who came before Me [as false messiahs and self-appointed leaders] are thieves and robbers, but the [true] sheep did not hear them. [9] I am the Door; anyone who enters through Me will be saved [and will live forever], and will go in and out [freely], and find pasture (spiritual security). [10] The thief comes only in order to steal and kill and destroy. I came that they may have *and* enjoy life, and have it in abundance [to the full, till it overflows].

His sheep know His voice and they know His. Hearing God's voice and following Him is a telltale sign of your sealed salvation. Jesus repeats himself here saying the same message in the first. Whenever scriptures are repeated, it reinforces the importance of a message. It's also important to note that we are commanded to listen and follow Him.

> [11] [c]I am the Good Shepherd. The Good Shepherd [d]lays down His [own] life for the sheep. [12] But the hired man [who merely serves for wages], who is neither the shepherd nor the owner of the sheep, when he sees the wolf coming, deserts the flock and runs away; and the wolf snatches the sheep and scatters *them*. [13] The *man runs* because he is a hired hand [who serves only for wages] and is not concerned about the [safety of the] sheep.

We have already looked at what makes Jesus a Good Shepherd, in these verses we learn that a bad shepherd is more selfish and is not willing to lay his life down for the sheep.

> [14] I am the Good Shepherd, and I know [without any doubt those who are] My own and My own know Me [and have a deep, personal relationship with Me]— [15] even as the Father knows Me and I know the Father—and I lay down My [very own] life [sacrificing it] for *the benefit of* the sheep. [16] I have [e]other sheep [beside these] that are not of this fold. I must bring those also, and they will listen to My voice *and* pay attention to My call, and they will become [f]one flock with one Shepherd. [17] For this reason the Father loves Me, because I lay down My [own] life so that I may take it back. [18] No one takes it away from Me, but I lay it down voluntarily. I am authorized *and* have power to lay it down *and* to give it up, and I am authorized *and* have power to take it back. This command I have received from My Father."

Jesus makes it clear in these verses that having a deep personal relationship with Him is not just what he desires, but He was willing to die for it. His heart's desire is for His sheep to follow Him and be blessed.

Jesus voluntarily laid his life down for you. What would it mean for you to lay your life down for Him? While some are called to lay down their physical lives for the cause of Christ, I believe this is addressing laying down of your days, thoughts, decisions, and priorities in favor of His. It is a dying of yourself that Jesus is calling you to so you may have the ideal life that God has for you. You must also lay your life down voluntarily for Him and for others to become who God sees you as already. The ones who do this are His sheep, and they know His voice and follow Him. Are you one of them?

Key Lessons from *A Shepherd Looks at Psalm 23*[13]

Phillip Keller wrote *A Shepherd Looks at Psalm 23* in the 1950s. In his younger years, he was a shepherd in Africa. Keller broke down each verse in Psalm 23 and gave scriptural and cultural insights on sheep and shepherding to clarify what David was really talking about when he penned this Psalm.

Sheep are among the most helpless animals ever created. They have no defense mechanisms. They cannot take care of themselves and they require meticulous care to survive. Sheep are incredibly fearful, timid, stubborn, and stupid. They have mob instincts in that if one panics they all begin to panic. Sheep have no sense of direction and without guidance will always get themselves in trouble.

God specifically created you as an object of His affections. His heart desires to care, guide, protect and defend you. He knows the safe places to lead you. All you have to do is follow Him. Sheep that are happy and healthy can only be so if they are being cared for by a good Shepherd. The same is true for you.

The Father chose you and called you by name to be one of His flock. The Good Shepherd delights in caretaking you and does so with perfection. Your job is to acknowledge His leadership and follow Him.

Shepherds Care, Guide, Protect, and Defend

> V1. The LORD is my Shepherd [to feed, to guide, and to shield me], I shall not want.

The love letter that the Lord gave me in 1979 included the words utterly, satisfied, content, fulfilled, and loved. This is what it means to

---

[13] *A Shepherd Looks at Psalm 23* by Phillip Keller, reprinted by Zondervan publications (1977)

not want. When you follow the Good Shepherd, you are led perfectly through the challenges of life under His guidance, protection, and strength.

> John 10:10 The thief comes only in order to steal and kill and destroy. I came that they may have *and* enjoy life, and have it in abundance [to the full, till it overflows].

The world encourages 'self-improvement', but the Lord knows that satisfaction and fulfillment are only found in Him. God only wants the best for you, and He knows that only He can lead you to it safely.

The Good vs the Bad Shepherd

There is a distinct razor-sharp earmark cut into every sheep. The carved symbol brands the sheep by its owner. This is so, at a distance people will know the owner of the sheep.

When you are saved, a spiritual tattoo on your heart marks you for Jesus. That tattoo can never be removed. It seals you until the day of salvation.

> John 10:28-20 [28] And I give them eternal life, and they will never, ever [by any means] perish; and no one will ever snatch them out of My hand. [29] [a]My Father, who has given *them* to Me, is greater *and* mightier than all; and no one is able to snatch *them* out of the Father's hand.

Without even seeing the earmark, you can tell if the sheep has a good shepherd or a bad one just by looking at it. If the shepherd has not given good care, guidance, and protection the sheep will not be healthy. When you try to follow your desires and direction, you become your own bad shepherd. It is impossible to compete with the Omni perfection of God. So, it's reasonable to assume that your way is not as wise as His way.

Proverbs 14:12 There is a way *which seems* right to a man *and* appears straight before him, But its end is the way of death.

Sheep need to keep moving forward. If they don't they wind up eating where they are eliminating waste and it makes them sick. Left to their own devices, sheep will go back and forth in the same place that they can dig ruts so deep they can't get out. This is the same for people. You must keep moving forward in life or your ruts can rob you of your destiny.

He Cares

Make Me Lie Down in Green Pastures[14]
https://youtu.be/W6ZEBhrBXr4

V2. He lets [makes] me lie down in green pastures; He leads beside the still and quiet waters.

---

[14] How to Make Me Lie Down in Green Pastors, film by Iroquois Valle Christian Church https://youtu.be/W6ZEBhrBXr4

In this film, a shepherd shows you the difference between making the sheep lay down and allowing the sheep to lay down in green pastures. What I liked about this film was the shepherd placing his arms across the chest of the sheep, kneeling, and laying with it on the ground. It is an interesting picture of what Jesus does for us when He has to make us lay down in green pastures.

The Lord made me lay down in green pastures when I got my Lymes disease diagnosis. It is a season where God gets your attention and stops your current trajectory to create a pause where you can focus on Him.

The shepherd in the film shared that he needed to do this process with this sheep, Leah because she had somehow gotten sick. Had he not made her lay down in green pastures she could have lost her life. Has there been a time in your life with the Lord is making you lay down in green pastures?

There are four conditions required for sheep to be able to lay down in green pastures without being made to do so. They must be...

- free of fear,

- free from friction, tension, and anxiety,

- free from torment or aggravation, and

- free from thirst and hunger.

Only the shepherd can alleviate these conditions. The peace that surpasses understanding is not something that is externally focused. That peace is a gift from God that comes only from tuning into the indwelling Holy Spirit. When you follow God intently, He knows your every need and meets it perfectly.

Sheep can be free of fear when they are close enough to see their shepherd whose job is to protect them from predators. These livestock animals can compete for the shepherd's attention and feeding grounds causing tension and anxiety. We live in a culture where competition and relational conflict is everywhere. The Good Shepherd can easily help you understand your circumstances by showing you things from His perspective. This reframes your circumstances and leads to peace.

V5b. You have anointed and refreshed my head with oil, my cup overflows

Sheep are constantly tormented by insects. Particularly irritating are these bugs that climb up the nostrils of the sheep and lay eggs creating maddening headaches that cause the sheep to continually bang their heads against fences to try to find relief. Additionally, their thick wool can house torturing parasites that create pain and constant itching. Sheep are dipped into vats of an oil concoction that not only alleviates the discomfort but also repels the bugs to prevent the condition.

This dipping process reminds me of baptism. Go into the water without the ability to fend off these aggravations and rise out of the water with the ability to avoid and deal with them better. Oil is a substance that when prayed over can have the material presence of God remain in it. It is used to pray for healing and also represents God's anointing presence. Along with breath, wind, fire, and water, oil is associated with the Holy Spirit.

Distractions, worries, irritations, and physical ailments can prevent you from being able to live the life God has for you. The solution is abiding. In God's presence, the material substance of his anointing sticks on you. The more you abide with Him the more of His anointed protection will be upon you. Spending time in the word of God will wash your mind and purify your thoughts so you may agree with God's truth and have His strength and comfort.

> Philipians 4:8 Finally, [a]believers, whatever is true, whatever is honorable *and* worthy of respect, whatever is right *and* confirmed by God's word, whatever is pure *and* wholesome, whatever is lovely *and* brings peace, whatever is admirable *and* of good repute; if there is any excellence, if there is anything worthy of praise, think *continually* on these things [center your mind on them, and implant them in your heart].

He Guides

> V3. He refreshes and restores my soul [life]; He leads me in the paths of righteousness for His name's sake

Sheep are the most defenseless of all livestock animals. They have no sharp teeth or claws, they lack a sense of direction and they cannot clean themselves. They are absolutely dependent on the shepherd for their care.

David was a shepherd in a dry parched land. Philip Keller was a shepherd in Africa, in a similar climate as David. Water for the sheep was a key component of their health. It was interesting for me to learn that dew is the purest water in the world. Sheep can exist on merely the dew from the early morning and the late evening found on the blades of grass. The shepherd would wake the sheep during these prime times so they would have the hydration needed for the entire day. And when he would lead them to brooks of water, he would make sure that it was clean so no sheep would get sick. The Good Shepherd knows the way and provides the best water for the flock.

The Living Water

> John 7:37-39 [37] Now on the last and most important day of the feast, Jesus stood and called out [in a loud voice], "If anyone is thirsty, let him come to Me and drink! [38] He who believes in Me [who adheres to, trusts in, and relies on Me], as the Scripture has said, 'From his innermost being will flow *continually* rivers of living water.'" [39] But He was speaking of the [Holy] Spirit, whom those who believed in Him [as Savior] were to receive *afterward*. The Spirit had not yet been given, because Jesus was not yet glorified (raised to honor).

Believers have the Holy Spirit dwelling inside them. He taps you into the flow of Living Water which is accessible to you 24/7. The flow connects you to God's mind, will, and emotion, and contains the supernatural power needed to live according to God's will and plans for you. The Lord described it to me once as like electricity. An object, like a toaster, for example, requires electricity to perform its purpose. Unplugged, it is dormant and impotent to accomplish its intended purpose. When we are not continually connected to the Living Water, the Holy Spirit within us, we are not accomplishing our intended purpose. Abiding in the Living Water is following Jesus' guidance as a lifestyle.

Jesus Shares How to Follow

> *To follow Me may seem like living in an opposite world. But My Scriptures clearly show you the way. Love is an act of obedience, a deliberate decision to follow My lead and not go your own way. This is always for your absolute best.*

> *It is a process of peeling back the onion layers of 'you' and all that gets in your way. Begin by letting go of the easy things*

93

first, like something that you know is out of your depth. And then with more time with Me, you'll move along to areas of surrendering deeper things, and the more you trust Me you will surrender even the familiar things.

Following Me means being willing to look different than the world. Standing up for righteousness in an unrighteous culture can be hard and takes courage. Humility is like a light that casts out your pride and sets you free from its shackles. I cannot come near pride. When you behave in prideful ways you remove yourself from My protective umbrella.

Living apart for Me is bondage. Freedom is only found under My perfect care. When you learn how to surrender to My will by letting go of your own, there is room for simply hearing and allowing Me to direct your paths more closely. When you choose otherwise it creates a static and it's difficult for you to hear and see Me clearly.

Stop asking 'why' when things are challenging for you and begin asking Who is my God? Learning how to cooperate with My will aligns you with My plans for you and leads you to the satisfaction and fulfillment and fruit-bearing that I have designed for you.

Ask yourself this question; whose will am I following here? Is it mine or God's? Adjust your path accordingly. Remember that My will is always for your best.

I AM the Good Shepherd, and I laid my life down for you. As one of My beloved sheep, follow Me and I will lead you to life abundant!

He Protects

V4. Even though I walk through the [sunless] valley of the shadow of death, I fear no evil, for You are with me; Your rod [to protect] and Your staff [to guide], they comfort and console me.

In the Meet the Truth chapter we talked about coming to your senses. Left to your own devices, you can take yourself down very dangerous paths that are way off track of God's best for you. When you're going through really hard times, and trials, it's important to remember to go through them with God and not alone. He will lead you to places of safety, and greater intimacy with Him, and strengthen you by the lessons learned through them.

For the believer who dies, the valley of death is not the end, but a portal to the high ground of heaven and the perfect presence of God. God will use your most difficult times to help you help others work through similar ones. When I worked at Catholic Charities, I learned that virtually every alcohol and drug counselor was a recovering addict. And found that grief counselors had all survived tremendous grief stories in their lives. God never wastes any moment of your life. He is ever-present in your darkest times.

The rod and the staff protect and comfort. The rod is a perfectly carved spear for the shepherd. It is used to attack enemies and is a symbol of strength, power, and authority. Its purpose is to keep the sheep safe. The rod is never used to hurt the sheep but only its enemies.

As we learned in the last chapter Aaron's rod spoke of his authority as the priest of Israel. As a child of God, it represents your authority to call on God's name for all needs and pull down His power from Heaven.

When a sheep would wander off in a dangerous direction, the shepherd could fling the spear close enough to startle the sheep, drawing its focus back to the shepherd.

I remember the day the Good Shepherd used his rod to get my attention. It was the last day of 1985, the end of a miserable year for me. I was in an abusive relationship with a guy who verbally and physically abused me. As the daughter of the boss, I was underpaid, underappreciated, and didn't enjoy what I was doing at work. I had recently received a pamphlet about a master's degree in organization development, but it looked out of reach.

I was visiting a friend in Toledo for New Year's Eve when the Lord showed me my true identity as the Princess of the King of kings. At that moment, the veil was removed from my eyes, and I purposed in my spirit that I would not be mistreated in 1986. I had a renewed spirit about this next year.

On New Year's day, with renewed commitment, I left on a mission to break up with this boyfriend, and enroll in that master's program, trusting God to provide for it so that I could move out of the job as quickly as possible. On the drive, I got stopped by a police officer and got a ticket for speeding. I remember laughing, which confused the cop. I told him that it was okay, the enemy was just trying to rob me of my destiny, and no matter what 1986 would be a good year. Nice try Satan!

It was a good year. Three weeks later I was in Washington DC for the orientation of that master's program. Five months later George and I got together and six months after that, George and I were married. At the time of this publication, we will have been married 34 years! I got my destiny back!

The staff is used for the gentle care of the sheep. It is a symbol of love and concern., a tool of comfort gently tapping the sheep on their bellies to give them mild direction. Sometimes it was used to lift a sheep that was stuck in the pits or ravines. newborn lambs cannot be touched by human hands, so the staff hook lifts and brings them close to their mother for nursing.

The Good Shepherd uses his staff to gently show us the way. The encounters that you have with the Lord in this book series are a way for you to be gently guided by His voice.

> Isaiah 13:21 Your ears will hear a word behind you, "This is the way, walk in it," whenever you turn to the right or to the left.

He Defends

> V5. You prepare a table before me in the presence of my enemies.

For a shepherd in the time of David, this verse is not referring to a meal with enemies. The table here is a high plain, a flat area at the top of a mountain. This was the place that shepherds would lead sheep in the late summer and early fall. A few months before, the shepherd would go up to this high plain and look for dangers such as poisonous foliage or threatening animal dens. He would prepare the land, by removing dangers and creating fences to protect the sheep before they get there.

The Omnipresent Good Shepherd goes into your future and looks for dangers so that He may adjust your path in the present to avoid dangerous situations in the future. The closer you walk with Jesus, the safer you will be. Nothing escapes His eye or takes Him by surprise. He can equip you to handle anything you will need to face in the future.

When David shared with King Saul that he had killed the lion and the bear, we see how these experiences prepared him to face Goliath. He knew that his God was with him then and would be with him for this challenge too.

Even truly dangerous situations in the natural are no match for God's umbrella of protection when you are walking according to His will. The closer you walk in alignment with the Good Shepherd the more he can supernaturally defend you. There will be challenges and dangers, but remember that He is your Defender.

Proof you are Following the Good Shepherd

> V6. Surely goodness and mercy and unfailing love shall follow me all the days of my life, And I shall forever dwell in the house and presence of the Lord.

Properly managed sheep can be the most beneficial livestock. But on their own that can be the most destructive. They will eat things that will make them sick, get stuck in ruts, and lead other sheep astray.

Those that follow the Good Shepherd leave blessings behind them. When you think of your legacy, how will people remember you? Are you a person who leaves behind peace or turmoil? Are you known for your forgiveness or your bitterness? Will they remember you for your contentment and joy or your conflict and frustration? Ultimately are your decisions motivated by love or selfishness?

Sheep are known by their Shepherd. Those who follow the Good Shepherd will leave behind faith hope and love, encouragement and inspiration. Their lives will be marked with contentment, satisfaction, and fulfillment having been empowered and energized by God's presence and they will accomplish the purposes which He has for them.

Encounter the Good Shepherd

Lay down in Green Pastures

God will reveal an area to which He wants you to pay attention.

- Relax, breathe deeply and welcome God's presence.

- As your childlike self, meet Jesus in your special place and play with Him for a few minutes.

- Ask Him to show you a time where He needed to make you lie down in green pastures (a time where He needed to slow you down, take care of an issue where you were going off track, or when He got your attention)

- Let Him show you where He was and what He was doing in that season (maybe that season is now!)

- What does He want you to learn from this?

- Ask Him all the questions you need to understand what He is saying to you.

- Record it all in your journal.

Wandering Areas

Jesus will identify and give counsel about the areas for which you tend to wander off outside of His will and protection.

- Relax, breathe deeply and welcome God's presence.

- Meet Jesus as your childlike self in your special place and play with Him for a few minutes.

- Ask Him to show you the areas in your life where you tend to wander away from God's will.

- Capture it all in your journal

- Take one step of obedience according to His direction.

Anoint my head with oil

The purpose of this encounter is for Jesus to purify your thoughts and drench you in His anointed presence.

- Relax, breathe deeply and welcome God's presence.

- Meet Jesus as your childlike self in your special place and play with Him for a few minutes.

- Jesus with speak with you about an area of your life He would like to purify and anoint. He will anoint your head with oil.

- This will look different for everyone.

- Make sure you journal all areas He makes clear for you about your life and direction.

Write Your Story by **Francesca Battistelli**

https://youtu.be/eKcImiTxqKg

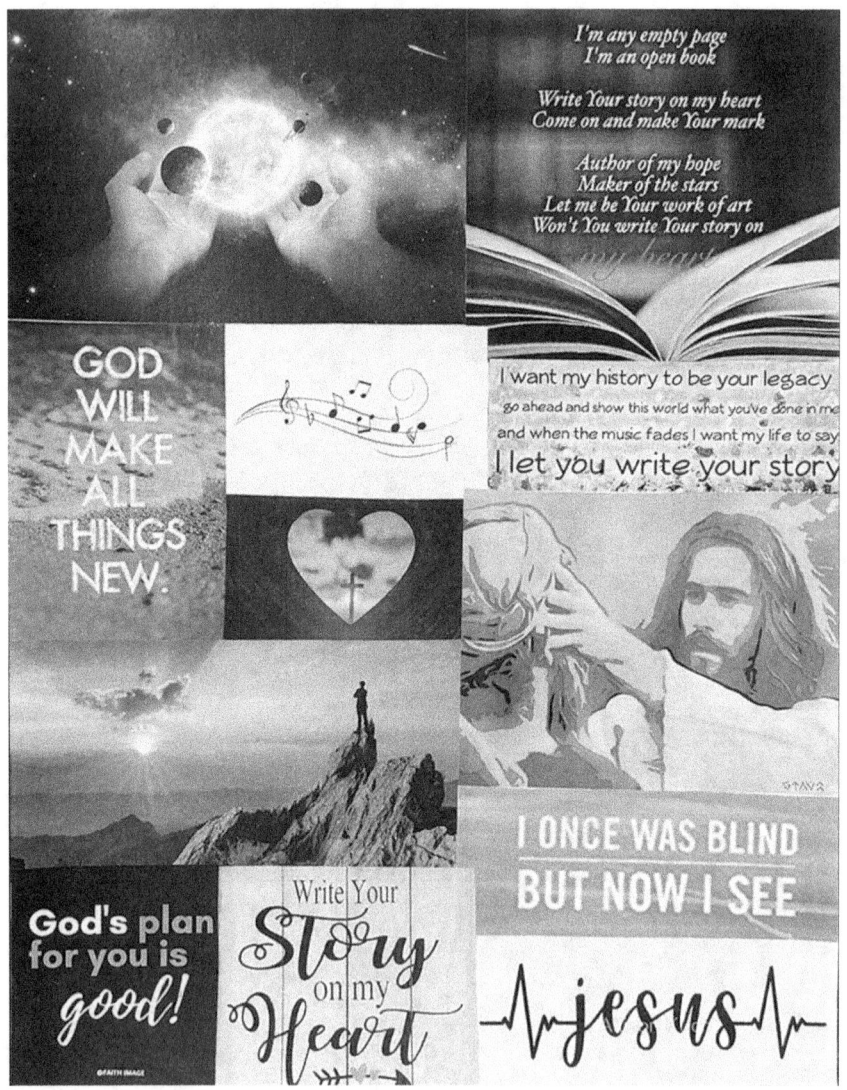

Meet the Author of your Story

We learn from this beautiful song from Francesca Battistelli that God is the source of the rhythm of your life. And that you must allow Him to make you His work of art. Your history is HIS story lived out in your skin.

> Hebrews 12:2 [looking away from all that will distract us and] focusing our eyes on **Jesus, who is the Author and Perfecter of faith** [the first incentive for our belief and the One who brings our faith to maturity], who for the joy [of accomplishing the goal] set before Him endured the cross, [a]disregarding the shame, and sat down at the right hand of the throne of God [revealing His deity, His authority, and the completion of His work].

The word author in Greek is *archégos* which means originator, founder, prince, and leader. The word perfecter is *teleiótés* which means finisher, completer, perfecter. Faith here is the word *pistis* which is the gift from God to believe, have trust, and faith for salvation and fruit-bearing service. Without God's gift of faith, you would not have the confidence to believe and walk out the plans He has for you.

God also works with you as your full partner for the completion of the purposes for which He has called you.[15]

My 'Doctor Who-Like' Dream

While taking my biblical dream interpretation class for my doctorate, I had a fantastical dream that felt very much like a "Doctor Who" episode. Here is a little context for those who are unfamiliar with the TV show. Doctor Who is a classic British science fiction television show that features a time-traveling superhero that protects the earth and other worlds from enemy aliens. Since the show's creation, there have been 13 actors who have played the main character, Dr. Who. This is made possible because he is an alien who looks like a human but can morph into other forms and continues to grow in character and capability as the stories and technology progress. To the outside world, the tardis spaceship looked like a common British police telephone box. Upon entering, it expands into a huge ever-changing interior spaceship.

I dreamt that I was on another planet, but it kind of felt like earth. People that seemed familiar to me in the dream but not familiar in waking life, were running. I had lost a trinket, a keychain that seemed important to me. I later remembered that it was a tardis keychain.

I found it and it showed me a portal. Gazing into the portal,, I saw a vision. It was like watching a movie on the screen and it showed the places where we needed to go. This gave me direction and I led the group toward this place that we needed to get to before the window of time would close. I was praying often, at every juncture for God to show me the way.

---

[15] Search on biblehub.com for Hebrews 12:2 https://biblehub.com/lexicon/hebrews/12-2.htm

We were running on rooftops, jumping from building to building. I felt like a rookie on a mission that had a lot of responsibility and pressure. When I woke up, I asked the Lord to help me understand the meaning of the dream.

> *You're feeling like a rookie right now on a great adventure as you learn these new ways of hearing My voice. In the dream, you prayed often for direction. This will be important for you to do every day as you gain experience in hearing My voice. You will try new things and sometimes you will fail, and sometimes you will succeed. But I will be with you the whole time. Your life is an adventure. I will give you direction and help you navigate one day at a time. Just like in the dream, you will suddenly know what to do and where to go. You will confidently move forward one step at a time. Don't worry about watching people that are watching you... I got you. I am the Author and Finisher of your faith.*

See God as the Author, See Your Life as a Story

To see God as the Author of your story, you must know yourself and see His influence on your life. This will require you to identify key lessons learned in your life that form your identity and clarify your purpose. Pay attention to the way God intersects your everyday life. This is your testimony. Noticing these things helps you learn how to share what you have witnessed and experienced from God directly.

To help you see those things, let's identify your primary emotional needs and your motivational gift.

There are three types of gifts; motivational, ministerial, and manifestation gifts. It is helpful for you to understand each type of gift and assess yourself so you know how God created and uses you. We will break down these gifts over the next three chapters.

In this chapter, we will address your motivational gift. In the Meet the Waymaker chapter, we will address your ministerial gifts. And, in the Meet the Supernatural Provider chapter, we will address the manifestation gifts of the Holy Spirit.

> 1 Corinthians 12:4-6 [4] Now there are [distinctive] varieties of *spiritual* gifts [special abilities given by the grace and extraordinary power of the Holy Spirit operating in believers], but it is the same Spirit [who grants them and empowers believers]. Manifestation
>
> [5] And there are [distinctive] varieties of ministries *and* service, but it is the same Lord [who is served]. Ministerial
>
> [6] And there are [distinctive] ways of working [to accomplish things], but it is the same God who produces all things in all *believers* [inspiring, energizing, and empowering them]. Motivational

We will address the motivational gifts later in this chapter.

Why is Sharing your Story Important?

The word gospel is *euaggelion* (yoo-ang-ghel'-ee-on) which translated means good news. The Gospels of Matthew, Mark, Luke, and John are the stories of what these disciples saw and heard from Jesus as they walked with Him day by day.

Every believer has been given the opportunity and the capability to walk with Jesus personally day by day. You are learning how to do that in this book series. When you share your story like Jesus' disciples did you show people the way to the faith hope and love that is found in Jesus Christ?

Sharing your story is the most effective way to evangelize because no one can argue with your story. Many people try to intellectually argue with people to lead them to salvation. This is not how Jesus did it. The Lord lives in your heart, not your head. And even the wisdom to understand the Scripture comes from heart knowledge gained by tapping into the Holy Spirit.

When you live a life that reflects the light and love of the Lord Jesus Christ, people will want what you have. Let's look at a life whose story does just that.

Hans Poley's Life Story

What you are about to read was a homework assignment for me in my doctorate when I was taking a creative writing class. Here was the assignment instruction: as an exercise in stirring your imagination, take a famous figure that you admire and think about what their life might have been like. Have them give you a tip on how to live your Christian life. Allow the Holy Spirit to lead the way to enlighten you on this assignment. (NOTE: I received this from the Holy Spirit and not from the spirit of Hans Poley in this exercise. The Bible does not encourage seeking to consult with spirits of the dead. This creative exercise was about asking the Holy Spirit to help me understand something from the perspective of one of the saints. The Lord can speak to us in any form He wishes, including a donkey!)

I think it's beneficial for you to have the context of the assignment before reading this encounter by watching a film clip from a movie based on the life of Hans Poley called *Return to the Hiding Place.* [16]

---

[16] Return to the Hiding Place trailer https://bit.ly/3duD2kr
And information about the movie https://en.wikipedia.org/wiki/Return_to_the_Hiding_Place

Return to the Hiding Place – Film Clip

https://bit.ly/3duD2kr

In a journaling vision, I saw myself as Hans, disguised as an older lady riding a bicycle through the Dutch cobblestone town. On this occasion, the mission was to receive a list of names, places, and addresses for which the Nazis were intending to pick up the next families. I felt my heart racing with nervous anxiety while riding through this town, passing Nazi soldiers on the street corners.

At the next glimpse, I felt like I was Hans distracting a guard by having a conversation and showing him fake papers so that the family who the guard had come to take away would have enough time to run away. I felt Hans's sweaty palms and nervous anxiety but worked hard to stay calm on the outside as I (he) spoke in perfectly accented German.

In the third glimpse, Hans and I were sitting on the hallway steps of Cory Ten Boom's house, and I asked him some questions. His answers are in italics.

You were still a teenager when you joined The Resistance. What made you want to do that?

It's one thing to hear a statistic about people being taken off to the camps, it's another thing to look into the eyes of those being taken away or their family members and see their sorrow and pain. I simply could not stand by and do nothing.

The work was dangerous and nearly all teen Resistance Army members were eventually killed. How did you cope with the danger, of being such a young man, and why do you think you are one of the only survivors?

The very safest place anyone can be used to live inside the will and calling of the Lord. I felt God's protection every day. Some days I believe He made me invisible to the enemy so I could accomplish what He wanted me to. He placed me where He needed me and equipped me to do what He wanted me to do each day.

There was a lot of joy in our success and a lot of suffering as well. The Lord even showed me his favor when I got to the concentration camp. On the day of my scheduled execution, the Lord caused the doctor to write a note that said that I had TB. The guards simply let me walk out of the camp a free man. Even a dead body with TB was a death sentence for anyone near it. I learned that this doctor's wife was one that I had helped to safety. His action was one of gratitude.

Those who gave their lives in the Resistance were blessed. The Lord rewards in heaven far more than any costs paid on earth for obedient service. One of the definitions of love is to be willing to lay down your life for someone else's. Jesus paid this price for us. Every believer should be willing to pay the same price for Him. To follow Christ into danger is not heroic. It's the minimum response of gratitude for what He has done for us. The heavenly reward is worth the price paid!

For many years I had no idea why I was a survivor and why the Lord spared me when my number came up for execution as He had not done for my comrades. But I believe the reason is that He wanted the story of the Resistance told. It was not just my story. It was the story of many who fought for the truth in the face of evil. It was not until that story was told that God took me for my heavenly reward. (Hans died in 2003).

What advice do you have for me?

The Lord will ask you to do things in your life that you find scary, dangerous, or challenging. Obey His voice and He will protect you. True satisfaction comes from living a God-honoring and obedient life. He will always equip you for every challenge.

Hans Poley was alive when this film was being created but died before seeing it completed. The special features of the DVD include an interview with him.

Know Yourself Part 1

In a Bible study called 'Unlocking Your Story',[17] Lance Wallnau looks at four emotional drivers that affect temperament and two additional factors that separate those who accomplish more for the kingdom from those who do not. I believe that this model was originally released by Tony Robbins, but Wallnau was able to see it through the lens of Kingdom purposes, which is why we are looking at it here.

Four Emotional Drivers and Two Enhancers

An emotional driver is another way of saying what makes you comfortable. There are four distinct emotional drivers. As you read

---

[17] https://s3-us-west.amazonaws.com/lwmproducts/Unlocking+Your+Story+Bible+-Study+Notes+Parts+1_2_3_4.pdf

through these, select one that you believe is your primary comfort, and another as a secondary one. It's fine if you don't have a second one.

- **Certainty** - These are people who love constancy, security, and safety. Facts and details assure them and can make them feel more comfortable. They understand cause-and-effect metrics and are secure when they can predict outcomes.

- **Uncertainty-**Those with this emotional driver are comfortable with change, new circumstances, and are stimulated by adventures. They love the thrill of possibilities and thrive in chaos. They enjoy pondering possibilities and tend to be creative and spontaneous.

- **Significance-** These people feel most at home when they can show their uniqueness and value in a circumstance. They do not need to look like everyone else and like to be independent of the rest of the pack.

- **Connection/Love-** Those with this driver need to feel closeness or union with others. They like to connect with people on deep levels.

These emotional drivers motivate you at a very core human need. If you are in a relationship with someone who does not share at least one of these emotional needs in common with you, your relationship may be toxic. Chemistry and connection are not the same as the former are physical and the latter are emotional.

High fruit-bearing Christians, those who accomplish great things for the Lord, develop in these two additional areas. Wallnau calls them enhancers.

- **Growth-** When a person has a heart for growing, the Lord sanctifies, and disciplines your emotional drivers. Too much of an emotional driver becomes a deficit. Let's take significance for example. If your need for significance is self-motivated, you can become prideful in your uniqueness and try to be famous, but not for godly reasons. If you have a heart for growth, the Lord will work on your humility and refocus your purpose off yourself and onto Him. You must be willing to grow and allow the Lord to maximize the effectiveness of your emotional drivers and minimize their potential deficits.

- **Contribution-** When the purposes in your life begin to reflect the heart of God and not your own will, your priority shifts to wanting to make a difference for others.

The Bible is filled with stories of how God takes people with overextended emotional drivers, sanctifies them, and moves them forward. Peter was a man with high uncertainty needs. He was the one who is willing to step out onto the water with Jesus. He also had a high significance need that was founded on pride.

> Matthew 26:33-35 ³³ Peter replied to Him, "Though they all fall away because of You [and doubt and disown You], I will never fall away!" ³⁴ Jesus said to him, "I assure you *and* most solemnly say to you, this night, before a rooster crows, you will [completely] deny Me three times." ³⁵ Peter said to Jesus, "Even if I have to die with You, I will not deny You!" And all the disciples said the same thing.

Even after Jesus told him he will deny Him, Peter defends his vow. Pride came before that fall. But only 50 days later, Peter's purpose was clear, and he had the power of the Holy Spirit that allowed him to bring more than 5,000 people to the kingdom in two sermons. His focus shifted off himself and onto God's people and His plan for them.

The Lord will sift you like wheat to sanctify your life and clarify your purpose.

Know Yourself Part 2

The first way that the Lord connects you with your purpose is to give you vision to see the needs for which He wants you to meet.

> 1 Corinthians 12:6. ⁶ And there are [distinctive] ways of working [to accomplish things], but it is the same God who produces all things in all *believers* [inspiring, energizing, and empowering them].

The Lord helps you see the needs of people through a unique lens. There is usually only one primary motivational gift. Remember this is not just about *how* you serve but a way to see *who* God wants you to serve. It will come from pondering such questions as; what and who do I seem to care about? And, what type of needs do I notice?

As you look through the list below make a self-assessment of your primary and secondary focuses. For more information about each gift, look up the verse that associates with it.

Motivational Gifts and your Self-Assessment

- **Prophesy-** God will show you the hearts of people that need to connect with God personally. He will give you the words that will uplift, encourage, and draw them closer to God. *Romans 12:6, 1 Corinthians 12:10.*

- **Service/Help/Hospitality- God helps you** recognize practical needs so you may help in meeting them. This kind of person notices the homeless person on the street and stops to give them a hand, or sees the person struggling to lift grocery bags, and runs to the rescue. People with this gift will do whatever it takes to help people in need. See *Romans 12:7, 1Peter 4:9-10*

- **Teaching-** This is the person whose heart burns for helping people understand God's Word and ways. God allows these people to make complicated things easy to understand to help people apply them to their lives. They build up, unify and help people to mature in the body of Christ. See 1 *Corinthians 12:28, Romans 12:7, Ephesians 4:11*

- **Exhortation/Encouragement-** This is the person who senses people's emotional needs with a hug, or a shoulder to cry on. They come alongside other believers with encouragement, comfort, consolation, and counsel to help them grow to be all that God intends for them. People with this gift are motivators of faith and God gives them the exact words for each circumstance that will help people feel better. See *Romans 12:8*

- **Giving-** People with this filter serve with selfless generosity, a willingness to share all material resources they have liberally and joyfully without the thought of return. These people are supporters of God's agendas. See *Romans 12:8*

- **Administration/Organizing-** People with this gifting filter see when a group needs structure or leadership and step in to offer help. The ability to lead and steer the body of Christ toward the accomplishment of God-given goals by planning, organizing, and supervising others. They can lovingly keep people on task and move them toward long-term goals. See *1Corinthians 12:28*

- **Mercy-** Those with this gifting see the needs to care for people. They step in empathetically giving help to those in need. People with this gift advocate for and serve with love to help alleviate pain and distress. See *Romans 12:8*

  Romans 12:6-8, "[6] We have different gifts, according to the grace given to each of us. If your gift is prophesying, then prophesy in accordance with your[a] faith; [7] if it is serving, then serve; if it is teaching, then teach; [8] if it is to encourage, then give encouragement; if it is giving, then give generously; if it is to lead,[b] do it diligently; if it is to show mercy, do it cheerfully."

Lessons from your Ups and Downs

Every life has its ups and downs. The Lord promises that there will be trouble in this life. Some people persevere past their challenges and others wallow and get stuck by them. The ones who remain stuck forfeit their kingdom impact and live below the abundant life for which God has called them. Those who live stuck live in circles, while those who persevere live in ever-reaching cycles.

Do you live in circles or cycles?

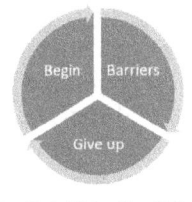

80% of Body of Christ will not fulfill their destinies because they do not access the Power of the Holy Spirit to accomplish their divine destinies. They make the barriers bigger than God.

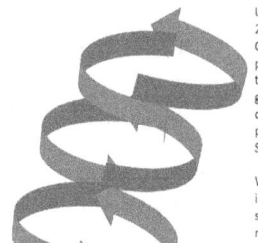

Unfortunately, only 20% of the Body of Christ tend to really persevere through the challenges and go for their divine destinies by the power of the Holy Spirit.

We are living in an important Kingdom season and God needs all of us to step into our callings!

The enemy's number one goal is to keep you from your destiny. If he can keep you focused on your challenges, frustrations, and the pains and limitations of this natural world, he can hold you back from your destiny.

John 10:10 The thief comes only in order to steal and kill and destroy. I came that they may have *and* enjoy life, and have it in abundance [to the full, till it overflows].

Tires that spin stuck in the mud dig themselves deeper and make it even harder to get out. The same is true for your trials. When you fix your eyes on the challenges, they grow within you. When you fix your eyes on Jesus, He grows within you. This is the secret to getting through difficult times. Understand that there is a lesson in your challenge and look to Jesus to pull you out of the mud. When you fix your eyes on Jesus, He will teach you lessons that pull you back up and move you forward. This is what it looks like to live in a cycle.

Because we are living in this Kingdom era, moving ever closer to the return of the Lord Jesus Christ, our cycles will be shorter. Difficult times are like the contractions a mother feels while laboring for a baby. The mom keeps her eyes on the baby, not the pain. She knows that for the joy set before her, it's all worth it.

> Hebrews 12:2 [looking away from all that will distract us and] focusing our eyes on Jesus, who is the Author and Perfecter of faith [the first incentive for our belief and the One who brings our faith to maturity], who for the joy [of accomplishing the goal] set before Him endured the cross, [a]disregarding the shame, and sat down at the right hand of the throne of God [revealing His deity, His authority, and the completion of His work].

Jesus kept His eye on the prize of our salvation and endured the cross to birth our freedom and access to the Father. How you choose to handle your challenges is key to whether you will fulfill your destined calling.

How to learn from the cycle

Dream	Distress	Develop	Demonstrate	Upgrade
Receive a prophetic promise from God and see a glimpse of what He has for you. As you picture this future you are filled with excitement and possibility! You have clarity of destiny.	Challenges and trials come your way and you question the vision and calling. Trials wear you down and you begin to take your eyes of the call. You can choose to stay stuck or press through.	The Holy Spirit allows you to see things from His perspective and you begin to align with His will, You understand the lesson in the trial. Refiners fire begins to humble and mature you.	Your eyes Are back on Jesus and you can See the dream again. You see how the trial prepared you for the next step toward the dream. You have learned the lessons of the season.	Learning What you needed to in the season has prepared you for an upgrade of anointing and moved you along the path of your divine destiny.

There is a process for each cycle. Let's break down what happens during a cycle. You begin with a vision, or dream from the Lord. He puts something big on your heart for you to do. Something to impact the people for whom He has made you see a need. You can see yourself using the skills and abilities that He has grown in you to meet that need. This dream will always be big and it will be inspiring, exciting, and scary.

For some, the dream starts subtly with thoughts or pictures of the possibility of a ministry, service, book, or population of people. You see hopeful pictures and you see yourself doing something. Many push these ideas away, but they come back every once in a while until they begin to occupy your mind quite a bit.

For others, the call comes like a freight train. As I shared in my *Clips that Move Mountains* book, I had no plans to become an author until I received a two-hour download from God with the book title, concept, and images of film clips in the book. One day it wasn't there, and the next it was all I could focus on.

So, it begins with a dream. Then, the challenges come. It's out of your comfort zone and people around you are not always supportive. The enemy will come against you and may distract you from your purpose with an illness, injury, persecution, or just plain busyness. How you handle that phase will either kill your dream, delay it, or move you toward it.

Here is what Jesus had to say about the dream:

I know how things will turn out. When you watch a movie or sports game on TV or read the novel before someone else has read it or seen it, you know how it's going to turn out. You could spoil the ending by sharing the ending. Telling them or not telling them doesn't change the outcome. It may change whether they want to read the book or see the event. Telling someone the story is worth seeing a reading, or that it's inspiring or exciting may make them want to see it. But telling them too much will likely influence the decision to see or read it.

I give glimpses of the future for this very same reason. I want you to know just enough to want more. I want to engage you, encourage you, or even warn you about the things that are coming so that you are on your toes and can confidently step into the future I have for you. When I tell you that millions will be blessed to grow by your ministry, it is not to puff you up with pride. It is so you will believe Me for the plans I have for you and stay the course and abide. I give you just enough to keep you inspired. And I don't give you too much or too little.

I know how this thing turns out. Believe Me. The Word is clear about what will happen at the end of time. You have your part to play in helping people, and I have all that you need to be ready for that eventuality. Stay the course and abide in Me. These things will happen for my Glory and My plans.

Overcomers move to the next phase and begin to align themselves with God's promises and preparations from the Word and direct encounters. Seeing yourself, your life and your calling through His eyes pull you back into alignment with His plans. When you allow challenges to purify you with God's refining fire, you emerge stronger.

Taking active steps of faith once again toward the dream is you demonstrating to the Lord that you have learned the lesson and allowed yourself to be pruned by the challenge. Pruning always cuts away what is hindering and allows for more life-giving energy to flow. You have passed the test and can handle an increased level of anointing toward God's dream destiny for you. Upgrades always come with an increase in God's anointing power.

It is unrealistic to expect that a dream can skip any low points and still get accomplished. Yet, people act so surprised when challenges come their way related to their dreams. Many people immediately think something is wrong when things get challenging. Or they even get mad at God because he's the one that gave them the dream in the first place. They can't understand why things are difficult. The Bible never promises easy, only that God will be with you every step of the way.

The difference between a person who lives in circles or cycles is their perspective. Do they look at the natural circumstance or do they look from God's perspective using the eyes and ears of their hearts to connect with Him? He will always provide the way through. People often pray for a way out. But lessons are learned when you get through them with God.

To choose to persevere through challenges or change, you need a compelling reason. A powerful "why" can pull you into your future.

Many people, for example, won't change their health habits until they have a health crisis. The crisis gives them a powerful why. When you prune your life by the sensitivity of hearing God's voice and knowing the word of God you become increasingly attentive to learning the lessons you need to succeed in a cycle.

Some key questions you want to ask when facing a challenge are; What do I choose to believe about this right now? Where are my eyes fixed? What has God said about this? Lord, what lesson do I need to learn to move through this situation? You can shorten your cycle seasons by addressing these questions with Jesus.

The call on your life was designed to succeed. Yet only 20% of people realize that they have the authority and the power to overcome any obstacle. You can tap into God's perspective and His power to be able to learn every needed lesson to accomplish the big dream that God has for you. Anchor your faith in your dream on this:

> Philippians 1:6 I am convinced *and* confident of this very thing, that He who has begun a good work in you will [continue to] perfect *and* complete it until the day of Christ Jesus [the time of His return].

Do not despise the testing. It is the place where you grow in maturity, humility, strength, and character. You cannot handle increasing levels of anointing and favor without the refiner's fire that builds your strong character. Your endurance gives you hope and qualifies you for the upgrade to your next level of anointing. Each level moves you closer to your destiny. Like the woman giving birth to a new child, hope comes when your eyes are fixed on Jesus. He increases the gift of faith which brings the power and endurance to move forward.

How has God written your Story?

Lessons from your Ups and Downs

Map your significant events could be related to spiritual, relational, career, family, mental, physical, emotional

Highs

Lows

Life in segments... could be decades, or just major life markers

Key questions... What did I learn; true or false in these seasons? How can I come into agreement with God's truth and plans for me? How can I allow God to use my high's and lows to prepare me for my divine destiny?

Looking at the grid above, you can divide your life into decades or just the highs and lows of your life story. You may pull from highs and lows related to your relationships, career, spiritual markers, health, etc.

What lessons did you learn from these highs and lows? What beliefs form your thinking about your identity based upon these significant highs and lows?

Meditate on these key questions with the Lord; What lesson did I learn true or false in the season? How can I agree with God's truth and plans for me now? How can I learn the needed lessons to prepare me for my divine destiny?

Take these issues to the Lord and have Him share with you why He allowed some of these things to happen. Ask God what you need to do to cooperate with the future that He has for you.

Witness and Testify- Sharing Your Kairos/Kronos Intersections

We live in chronological time here on earth. The Greek word for chronological time is *kronos.* It is limited to 24 hours a day, moving in one direction from birth until death. The Lord lives in timelessness, which in Greek is *kairos.* He was, is, and always will be all at the same time. We can't understand that. We get a sense of that when we encounter Him in our special places, and it can feel like many hours when it was only a few minutes.

As we navigate this earthly world as children of God, we are not limited by the natural laws as much as we may think when we are when we connect with Him. A kairos/kronos intersection is when God intersects your natural timeline and shows up supernaturally. When you lay hands and pray for God to heal something that doctors have declared as hopeless and you see a miracle healing, you have just witnessed a kairos/kronos intersection.

Seeing something happen makes you a witness. Telling someone that it happened is your testimony. The more time you spend with the Lord, the more you will witness His love, power, grace, and mercy. Telling people of these encounters is testifying to their validity. The terms witness and testify are used in courtrooms because they are key methods for the jury and judge to decipher the truth.

Key Steps to Share your Story

There are a few simple key questions you can ask yourself that will pull effective evangelistic stories from your life. Before we dive into them, I think it's important to note that your life is not just one story. Your life is too big and too complex to be just one story. For example, the Great Physician has healed my body seven times. Each time is a story that can be told to inspire someone who needs physical healing.

Your salvation story, the story of how God has moved you in your career and ministry, lessons from bad relationships or even lessons from near-death or scary circumstances provide excellent backdrops for explaining how the Lord showed up for you in your life and moved you forward. Simply thinking of these few questions will help you break down your life into pieces so that when you face somebody challenged with a similar situation, you can easily pull from your own life experience and move them toward Jesus.

The key questions that will help you tell your stories are;

- Where were you before Jesus? What was your life like, before He showed up?

- How did He show up? (You are meeting Him by his various Names in this book series. You are creating memories with Him as you learn to address issues in your life. These encounter stories add to your stories)

- What changed as a result of God showing up?

- How has your life changed as a result of God's direct influence?

- Why would somebody want that? (Share here the benefits of your life with Him since.)

This film clip from *King's Faith* does a beautiful job of showing how addressing these points in a few-minute conversation can powerfully share a story that leads people closer to God.

Tell your Story- King's Faith clip[18]
http://bit.ly/1ccNTVR

Could you see how Brendan easily shared his story with this group of young people? It is much easier than you think to share the good news of who God is in your life. That's what the Author of your story does best!

Encountering the Author of your Story

Your Motivational Gift –

- After spending some time in worship and playing with Jesus in the special place for a few minutes, then...

- Ask the Lord to show you or speak to you about your primary motivational gift.

- How has He revealed this gift through your life story?

- How do you plan to use this to guide you going forward?

Circles or Cycles-

---

[18] Tell your Story, Clip from *Kings Faith* http://bit.ly/1ccNTVR, by Nicholas Dibella

- After properly posturing your heart with the Lord, Ask Him these questions, allowing Him to show you in any way He chooses. Open the eyes and ears of your heart to receive the truth.

- Lord, speak to me about times when I get stuck in circles.

- How can I see you in the challenge more easily and choose to grow and develop so I can move to the next stage of your anointed plan for my life?

Lessons from my Ups and Downs-

- Prayerfully draw your story with the Lessons from our Ups and Downs chart.

- Then meet Jesus in your special place. Play with Him for a while and praise Him to properly posture your heart.

- Then ask the Lord to reveal insights related to the key questions on that chart.

Tell your Story-

- Prayerfully look at your ups and downs and meet the Author in your special place and ask Him to help you see a few areas in your life that you can make into short stories to share when people ask you about your life in Christ, or when you meet someone facing a similar challenge.

- Ask Him for insights about the lessons He had for you in those seasons. Allow Him to give you His perspective on them as you look back on those times and reflect on how they impact you now.

Waymaker by Sinach

https://youtu.be/n4XWfwLHeLM

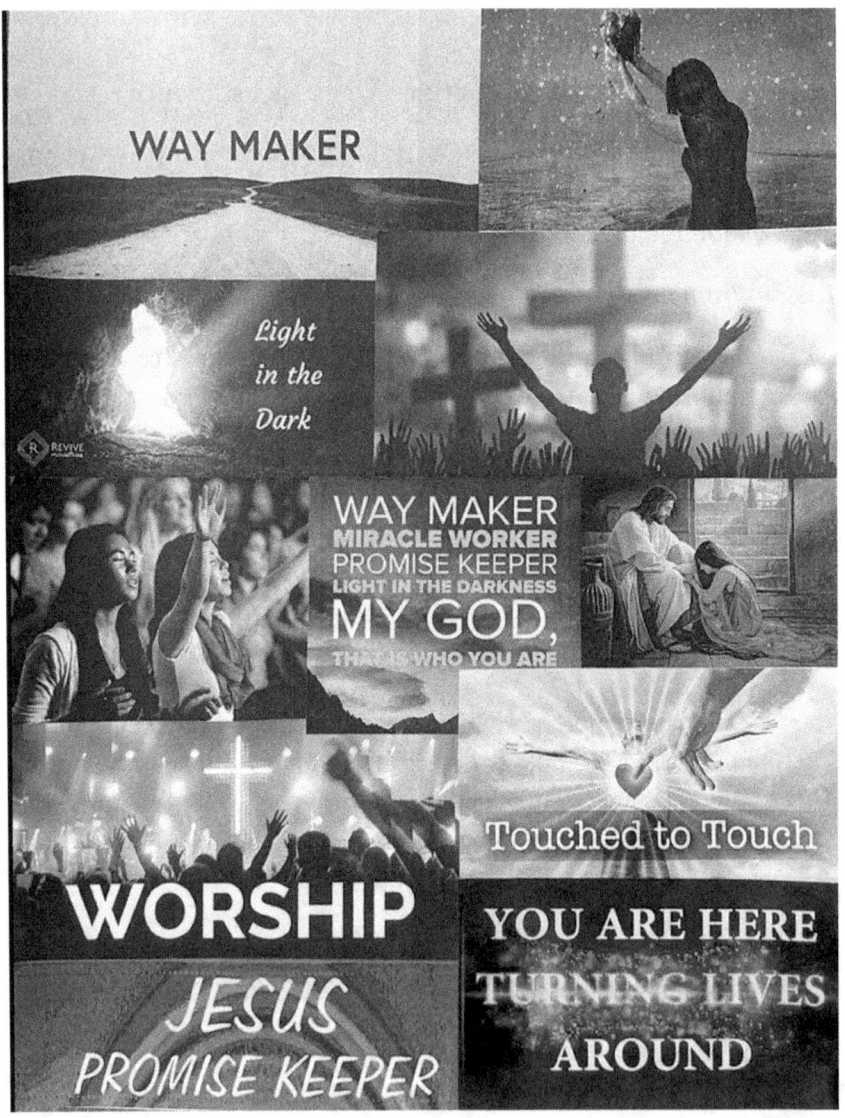

Meet the Waymaker

Nigerian Gospel Artist, Sinach wrote and released our lyric video song, *Waymaker* in 2015 popularizing this Name of God.[19] Since then, this song has been released by many artists and translated into more than 50 languages. It was an obvious choice for this chapter. It was after I finished my biblical research for this chapter that I realized how anointed this song is and how especially important its messages are for this time and season.

Who is the Waymaker?

There are verses in the Bible that show all three members of the Trinity as the Waymaker. Jesus declared Himself as the Way.

> John 14:6 Jesus said to him, "[a]I am the [only] Way [to God] and the [real] Truth and the [real] Life; no one comes to the Father but through Me.

Isaiah shows us how the Father is working on our behalf behind the scenes.

---

[19] https://en.wikipedia.org/wiki/Way_Maker

> Isaiah 45:15 (MSG) Clearly, you are a God who works behind the scenes, God of Israel, Savior God.

Part of the indwelling Holy Spirit's job description is to lead us. Notice here that we have to cooperate with that guidance.

> Romans 8:24 For all who are *allowing themselves to* be led by the Spirit of God are sons of God.

Each part of the Trinity plays a role as the Waymaker.

What is His purpose?

The enemy's sole purpose is to rob you of your destiny. Everything that Satan does is aimed at that goal. The Waymaker's purpose is the exact opposite. It is to ensure the complete execution of the Kingdom plan. Every Spirit-born believer has a divine destiny as part of God's plan. Not every believer will cooperate with that destiny. Unfortunately, many do not pick up their mantles and serve according to the plans God has for them.

> Philippians 1:6 I am convinced *and* confident of this very thing, that He who has begun a good work in you will [continue to] perfect *and* complete it until the day of Christ Jesus [the time of His return].

And the Lord will accomplish every word He promised in the Bible whether the whole body of Christ cooperates or not. If you are not willing to do your part, He will find someone else to step up. God's will prevails regardless. For this reason, some, like Billy Graham, were trusted to harvest tens of thousands of souls. It's not too late for you to rise to your destiny's fruit-bearing.

> Isaiah 55:10-11 ¹⁰ "For as the rain and snow come down from heaven, And do not return there without watering the

earth, Making it bear and sprout, And providing seed to the sower and bread to the eater,[11] So will My word be which goes out of My mouth; It will not return to Me void (useless, without result), Without accomplishing what I desire, And without succeeding *in the matter* for which I sent it.

How does He work?

There are two ways that the Lord directs you. He shows you what to do. And He will show you how. The 'how' includes the ways He wants you to accomplish His goals. Listening to God's voice for both types of specific directional guidance is critical to knowing the way to go. Let's look at a story in the Bible where we can see the Holy Spirit directing Paul and his camp in these ways.

> Acts 16:6-9 [6] Now they passed through the territory of Phrygia and Galatia, after being forbidden by the Holy Spirit to speak the word in [the west coast province of] Asia [Minor]; [7] and after they came to Mysia, they tried to go into Bithynia, but the Spirit of Jesus did not permit them; [8] so passing by Mysia, they went down to Troas. [9] Then a vision appeared to Paul in the night: a man from [the Roman province of] [a]Macedonia was standing and pleading with him, saying, "Come over to Macedonia and help us!"

We see in this story, that the Lord was stopping them to go in certain directions. Then sent a message to Paul in a dream giving Him the way to go.

Another example is when the Waymaker gave crystal clear instructions to Bezalel and Ohiliab, skilled craftsmen in all the arts, for the specific creative instructions for how to build every furnishing of the Holy Tent in the time of Moses. See Exodus 31 -36. These men received detailed instructions down to exact measurements of what the Lord wanted them to make.

God still works this way. I like to call them downloads. It's where you get a very clear instruction of what to say, do, write, or create directly from God. This is how Christian artists receive their lyrics and melodies, writers receive their words, painters their pictures or patterns, and scientists their discoveries, for example. You can tell an anointed work by how it makes you feel when you experience it. God inhabits all of His creation.

When does He show up?

One thing to understand about God's timing is that it is much more comprehensive and strategic than you can wrap your head around. We must remember that we are operating as part of a grand Kingdom plan. Imagine that you are one puzzle piece in a billion-piece puzzle. You are linked to many other puzzles but are not privy to the greater percentage of other puzzle pieces. For the timing to be perfect, the Waymaker is juggling the timing of an untold number of factors. While considering the factors you may be aware of, know that there are many more factors that you are unaware of that cause delays. Let's look at a story in the book of Daniel for a factor that caused a delay that we never think about. This is a conversation Daniel had with an angel.

> Daniel 10:4-17 (MSG) [4-6] "On the twenty-fourth day of the first month I was standing on the bank of the great river, the Tigris. I looked up and to my surprise saw a man dressed in linen with a belt of pure gold around his waist. His body was hard and glistening, as if sculpted from a precious stone, his face radiant, his eyes bright and penetrating like torches, his arms and feet glistening like polished bronze, and his voice, deep and resonant, sounded like a huge choir of voices.

7-8 "I, Daniel, was the only one to see this. The men who were with me, although they didn't see it, were overcome with fear and ran off and hid, fearing the worst. Left alone after the appearance, abandoned by my friends, I went weak in the knees, the blood drained from my face.

9-10 "I heard his voice. At the sound of it I fainted, fell flat on the ground, face in the dirt. A hand touched me and pulled me to my hands and knees.

11 "'Daniel,' he said, 'man of quality, listen carefully to my message. And get up on your feet. Stand at attention. I've been sent to bring you news.'

"When he had said this, I stood up, but I was still shaking.

12-14 "'Relax, Daniel,' he continued, 'don't be afraid. From the moment you decided to humble yourself to receive understanding, your prayer was heard, and I set out to come to you. But I was waylaid by the angel-prince of the kingdom of Persia and was delayed for a good three weeks. But then Michael, one of the chief angel princes, intervened to help me. I left him there with the prince of the kingdom of Persia. And now I'm here to help you understand what will eventually happen to your people. The vision has to do with what's ahead.'

15-17 "While he was saying all this, I looked at the ground and said nothing. Then I was surprised by something like a human hand that touched my lips. I opened my mouth and started talking to the messenger: 'When I saw you, master, I was terror-stricken. My knees turned to water. I couldn't move. How can I, a lowly servant, speak to you, my master? I'm paralyzed. I can hardly breathe!'

From the moment that Daniel prayed, the angel was dispatched to bring him a message. But was delayed. This angel needed the assistance of the Arch Angel Michael to be able to accomplish his mission. There are spiritual factors at play that can cause timing delays in our callings. It's also important to note that spiritual battles are happening with angels and demons related to your destined assignments. We will learn more about this in *Encountering the POWER of God:* Experience Jesus book 4.

Seeing the Waymaker

Past

I was a shy B/C student for my entire pre-college academic life. I did not like the left-brained academic expectations of learning by rote memorization. It was not how the Lord had wired me to succeed. This affected my self-esteem causing me to believe that I wasn't smart.

I was a dance major at Ohio University for only one semester. I took an experientially designed class on interpersonal communication that was a game-changer for me. To learn about nonverbal communication for example we were sent to the mall dressed normally for the time, and then again in rags, and once more as a hippie. We were to record people's reactions to us based on how we were dressed. Through these and many other practical interventions, I learned that experience was my best teacher and it influenced how I teach and learn ever since.

When it came time for me to go back to school for my Masters, I went to a new program at American University (AU) in Washington DC in partnership with a practitioners training organization, National Training Labs (NTL). The AU/NTL program was an experiment in experientially designed programming for the field of organizational development. It was one of only three such programs in this new field at the time in the nation.

One weekend a month for two years, I would drive to Washington DC, stay with another student in the program and our cohort of 22 students would practice the models and tools we had read about in our homework at home for the weekend. The program also required a six-month practicum where we consulted an organization using everything we were learning practically with a real company.

This experience further reinforced for me that experience is the way God teaches and works through me. Imagine my delight when I discovered Christian leadership University (CLU) that's foundational principle is to learn how to hear God's voice so He can be your actual One-on-one instructor using the very same skills that I am teaching you in this book series.

I want to share one more story about how the Waymaker showed up in my past and I only discovered it recently. Hindsight is 20/20 vision.

The only connection with Robin that I had with her was when we were eight years old children. My mother was a realtor and she brought me to Robin's house while she discussed listing it with her parents. The only thing I remember about that encounter was that Robin taught me how to blow a spit bubble at the end of my tongue.

Robin and I did not hang out with the same kids in school. But at the 40th high school reunion, I walked up to her to share my spit bubble memory. She asked me where I attended college. I told her Ohio University for all four years.

The story she shared with me about the reason for the question highlighted the Waymaker to me in such an interesting way. Robin arrived at OU and learned that I was supposed to be her roommate.

I arrived at OU and the housing people were perplexed because they had a record of housing payment but no actual assignment for housing for me.

They placed me in temporary housing with Valerie, who had decided late to attend the university. Valerie and I became best friends and stayed together. A month later when we moved to another dorm across campus. My connection with Valerie led to my salvation story. The boyfriend I had that was connected to the story of my salvation was introduced to me by Valerie.

Meanwhile, Robin was waiting for me to arrive at the room and went through some stages of hurt, anger, and eventual acceptance. She shared that she constantly looked for me on campus, initially to tell me off, and then to just want to know why I didn't wind up rooming with her.

She shared that she held some pain in her heart from that rejection and was glad to hear the real story. The strangest thing about needing to wait 40 years to learn that the Waymaker was directing my life in that season, was that her closest friend lived in the same dorm as where Valerie and I had lived in our second year on campus. She was even on the other wing of the same floor, and Robin spent a lot of time with her there. Yet, we never crossed paths. I used to see her friend quite a lot in the hallway or the bathroom. The Waymaker was charting my paths without me even knowing it even before I said yes to His gift of salvation.

Are there times in your life that you can think back on how the Lord was there directing and guiding you for something relevant for you to do now?

Future-

God goes into your future and prepares your connecting pieces of the Kingdom plan puzzle for you before you get there. I had been working at Parmadale/Catholic Charities for nearly a decade. I loved the many hats I wore as the Director of the Training Institute for Parmadale and Director of Organization Development for Catholic Charites in the Cleveland, Ohio Diocese. We were pulling together eight counties of services into one cradle-to-grave system of services. It was challenging work and we were making a difference. I pushed aside the feeling that God wanted me to leave that job and go out on my own as an Independent Consultant for about six months. I had already been there and done that. The marketing to stay working independently was brutal. At the end of 1999, I couldn't shake the calling anymore and I left that cushy job and set out on my own.

It was only a few weeks later that Lisa, a colleague from the County's Children's Service Department, and I wound up sitting at the same lunch table at a meeting. She was the new Director of the Family and Children's First Council. At that lunch, the door opened up for me to work with Lisa for 14 years! For six years, I worked with her to help streamline the services of fourteen public service organizations serving a common population. Then when she moved to the Cleveland Foundation, I worked for eight years with small tiny faith-based organizations delivering services to their communities as part of the National Faith-Based initiative. God prepared me with the role I had at Parmadale and Catholic Charities to serve not more than 35 different groups and organizations who themselves served tens of thousands of people through the re-connection made at one lunch.

There is another kind of impact that you won't even be aware of until you get to heaven. Remember the story of the skipping stones? Once the stone leaves your hand and multiplies, you can't see the ripples and multiplication it makes in the natural realm. Even small conversations that you have had with someone may have a deeper impact than you are aware of. The Lord sees it all and knows it all. I believe we will not even know until we get to heaven, or even until judgment day, what our true impact has been. This film clip that I originally shared in the *Clips that Move Mountains* book, still says it better than any I have seen yet.

Strangers Film Clip[20]
https://bit.ly/3yMfiie

Your impact is not limited to your lifetime. The Apostle Paul, for example, for his contribution by writing two-thirds of the New Testament, and his life example is still racking up heavenly rewards for his legacy for the Kingdom.

---

[20] Strangers Film by Igniter media https://bit.ly/3yMfiie

Present

The Word is filled with incredible stories of the Waymaker showing up in the lives of people, making a way where there seems to be no possible earthly way. Imagine being one of the Israelites being chased by Pharoah's soldiers on horses and chariots while standing on the beach of the Red Sea! Then the Lord created walls of water so more than two million of them walk across the dry ground. Then watching the water close over the soldiers after the last Israelite gets across! (See Exodus 14:1-30)

In researching this event, I found some fascinating insights about this miracle. [21] Knowing the location of the crossing which is now known as the Sanai Pennisula, the eight-mile journey across the bottom of the sea would have had walls of water 1,000 feet high. The amount of wind that would have required those walls to remain open for the 2/3 of a mile wide that it would have taken for all of them to cross, would have been like an unsurvivable tornado.

> Exodus 15:8 [8]"With the blast of Your nostrils the waters piled up, The flowing waters stood up like a mound; The deeps were congealed in the heart of the sea.

To congeal is to thicken, to change from liquid to solid, or to fix in place. So, God either literally froze the water into 1,000 feet high walls or froze the water in time, rendering it stuck in place where God moved them until He was ready to release the water again. What an incredible miracle to have experienced for the Israelites in their present reality!

Way of Escape

God has also promised to make a way to avoid temptation at the moment you need it.

---

[21] http://www.bibleplus.org/discoveries/redsea.htm Red Sea Crossing site re-discovery.

1 Corinthians 10:13 No temptation [regardless of its source] has overtaken *or* enticed you that is not common to human experience [nor is any temptation unusual or beyond human resistance]; but God is faithful [to His word—He is compassionate and trustworthy], and He will not let you be tempted beyond your ability [to resist], but along with the temptation He [has in the past and is now and] will [always] provide the way out as well, so that you will be able to endure it [without yielding, and will overcome temptation with joy].

How do you find your way of escape? Here are three tips:

1. Recognize that there will be one. God has promised in His Word that He will provide it. Look for it. Ask the Lord to show you where to look to find it. Sometimes it is the choice to not put yourself in a situation where the temptation will be there in the first place.

2. Choose God's choice. As we learned in the Good Shepherd chapter, Jesus said, My sheep hear My voice and they follow Me. Sometimes you know exactly what the way of escape is, and you just need to choose that way out.

3. Want the way out? Sometimes that means facing a fear or humbling yourself. To grow, you must be willing to turn and walk in God's direction. Surrendering your will to the Lord is the quickest way to overcome issues.

    Psalm 37:23 [23] The steps of a [good and righteous] man are directed *and* established by the LORD, And He delights in his way [and blesses his path].

Ministerial Gifts

We learn about the Ministerial Gifts that are also referred to as the Five-fold Ministry Gifts from Ephesians.

Ephesians 4:11-13 [11] And [His gifts to the church were varied and] He Himself appointed some as apostles [special messengers, representatives], some as prophets [who speak a new message from God to the people], some as evangelists [who spread the good news of salvation], and some as pastors and teachers [to shepherd and guide and instruct], [12] [and He did this] to fully equip *and* perfect the saints (God's people) for works of service, to build up the body of Christ [the church]; [13] until we all reach oneness in the faith and in the knowledge of the Son of God, [growing spiritually] to become a mature believer, reaching to the measure of the fullness of Christ [manifesting His spiritual completeness and exercising our spiritual gifts in unity].

Many limit the understanding of the ministerial gifts from Ephesians 4 to be only about the church you attend, or the small body or denomination for which you serve. With this understanding, those who do not have full-time positions in the church believe these gifts do not apply to them. But the church means the body of Christ inclusively. This means that every believer is needed to play these roles and sometimes different roles as needed.

The goal of these roles is to build up or equip the body of Christ to grow in maturity so we can unify to accomplish God's Kingdom plan. Roles played without being submitted to the Holy Spirit are dead works.

Let's look at all of these roles with a hand as a metaphor.

Apostle- The Thumb

The word apostle in the Bible is *apostolos* which means to be sent or commissioned by Jesus to represent Him to others. It means to have the authority and power of God to share the Gospel of Good News with the people. The original apostles walked with Jesus directly. All

Spirit-led believers are technically apostles, as we have the indwelling power of the Holy Spirit and are called to be the light in our dark generation. As you are learning how to do this in this book series, you too walk with Jesus directly and are empowered to be a leader over the ministry of your calling.

The Apostle is a foundational leadership role that encompasses the others. Apostles are messengers that lay the foundation for the other roles to work in concert. For this reason, people with this gift often are leaders in the team and may build churches, set up ministry services, and motivate people to work in unity toward the Great Commission.

Being sent doesn't need to mean to a foreign country. It can also mean right under your roof. As a parent, your job is to shine the light of God's truth in your family. Represent God well so that your children will come to know Him and grow in maturity.

The Apostle is the thumb because it is the only finger that touches all of the others. It has unique benefits for grasping and holding. As a leader, the Apostle works in cooperation with all of the other roles.

Prophet- The Pointer Finger

The word *prophétés* or prophet means to be an interpreter or sharer of the divine will of God. To prophesy is simply to speak what the Lord has said or shown you that is consistent with the Word of God. God speaks to each person directly for your edification, encouragement, and guidance. A person playing the role of Prophet is receiving messages that are meant to bless, uplift, or guide others. Sometimes these can be messages of warnings or conviction.

People acting in the role, always under the inspiration of the Lord are speaking out loud so that those who are not listening to the Lord directly will hear Him with their natural ears. Only trust prophetic messages that are consistent with the Word.

The Prophet is the pointer finger because he or she shows people the way the Lord is directing. They will speak whatever Christ chooses to speak for the purification and perfection of His church. This may be guidance, instruction, rebuke, warnings, or revelation.

Evangelist- The Middle Finger

The word for Evangelist in the Bible is *euaggelistés* which means the bringer of the Good News for salvation. It refers to the sharing of the complete message of God's gift of salvation. Whenever you share your story as we discussed in the last chapter, you are evangelizing. The very act of sharing the story is at the least a seed planted for salvation and at best, leading them to the way of salvation. Evangelists shine the light in the darkness and encourage people with the hope of eternal life both here and in heaven. It is a role that encourages, uplifts, and directs.

The middle finger stands the tallest in the hand and therefore has the farthest vantage point. They are charged to keep the team's eyes on God and His promises.

Pastor- The Ring Finger

We learned in the Meet the Shepherd chapter that the word pastor is *poimén,* the same word as a shepherd. Pastors, care for, guide, protect, and defend the people for which God has given them influence and authority. You play this role at work, at home with your family, and even with your friends.

The ring finger represents the pastor because of the commitment represented by the marriage ring, to the people for whom the Lord has called the team to serve.

Showing people that you care and reflecting the love of God and lending a hand when you see they need you is an example of playing this role circumstantially.

Teacher- The Pink Finger

Didaskó means to cause to learn. A teacher's role is to help people understand the truths of the Word and how to live out the faith by the power of the Holy Spirit. They know that it is important to connect with the Lord so He may make His plans and steps clear. You exercise this gift when you help someone connect with Jesus, teach a Bible study class, or share something that makes people understand the scripture.

While it may be the smallest finger in the hand, it is important for balance and strength. Without a clear understanding of Scripture, we would not have guidance. Teachers are represented by the pinky finger to signify the importance of grounding the team in the Word of God and making sure that the team accurately and honorably reflects the light of the love of God in the execution of the ministry.

The Five-Fold Ministry

The Lord never intended for us to accomplish our part of the Kingdom plan alone. The Five-Fold Ministry idea is that if you had a ministry team all led by the Holy Spirit, with all of these roles being played by people who were naturally gifted in those roles, you would have the complete package.

In his book, *The Five-Fold Effect*[22], Walt Pilcher uses a diagram to share the relationship that each role should ideally have related to the population for which they are serving.

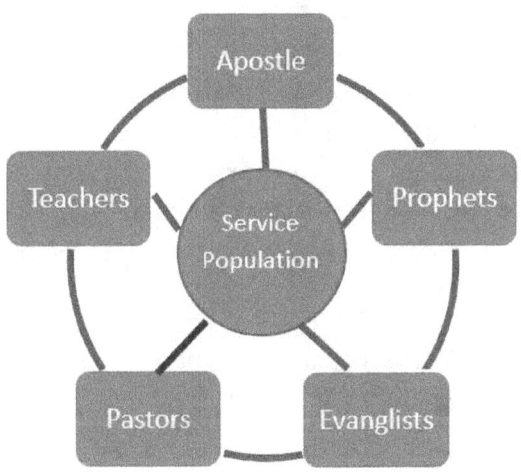

The team, under the inspiration of the ultimate leadership of the Holy Spirit, is equipped to bless the people for whom they are called to serve. This is because the Lord joins and knits together the people allowing each to play their part in moving the body of Christ forward toward God's plans.

When Christ is at the center of the team, whether it is inside the church or in the marketplace, all members will reflect God's nature

---

[22] *The Five-Fold Effect,* by Walt Pilcher, ©2013 by West Bow Press

and character in their service. They will be servant leaders; humble, surrendered to God, serving with selfless goals and Godly ambitions. They will set the tone of love and responsibility to the service population. This is God's vision for how we are to work in partnership with Him and others toward His Kingdom plan.

The Offices

To operate any of these roles at the level of an Office means that you have earned the trust of the Lord to receive higher levels of anointing in an area. The word in the bible closest to the concept of the office is *episkopos* which means overseer, supervisor, leader, a person called by God to "keep a keen eye" on His people. This word is used to describe a leadership or supervisory function related to the body of Christ. Elder and deacon are two such church-related roles that come to mind related to this idea.

> Acts 20:28 [28] Take care *and* be on guard for yourselves and for the whole flock over which the Holy Spirit has appointed you as overseers, to shepherd (tend, feed, guide) the church of God which He bought with His own blood.

You must seek the higher gifts and not the higher offices. Pride can enter in and throw you off God's course when what you want is to hold an office for personal reasons and not for God's purposes. Never try to be in an office for which the Lord has not elevated you. This is an open door for the enemy to mess with you. God won't let you carry a title for Him if you care about the title.

The enemy can recognize the traits of those God uses in higher offices even before you realize it yourself, and will try to use pride to keep you off track. Serving at an office level without God's anointing to do so removes you from God's guidance and protection. You can wind up hurting yourself and others in this situation. Do only what the Lord directs you to do. And your faithfulness and humility will earn you a higher office.

The whole reason God gifts you is so you can be a gift to others using the uniqueness of how He created you. Everything you do to serve God that is directed by and done with Him is anointed. When God is ready to elevate you, He tells you. He gives you glimpses, opens doors, and gives you higher assignments.

Don't believe God is unable to use you at a higher level because you are not working inside of a church. God is inside of you. Everywhere you go, He walks with you into the room. Simple humility and obedience move you to the higher places of service in the Kingdom plan.

What it takes to be the Head and not the Tail

> Deuteronomy 28:13 The LORD will make you the head (leader) and not the tail (follower); and you will be above only, and you will not be beneath, if you listen *and* pay attention to the commandments of the LORD your God, which I am commanding you today, to observe them carefully.

At the same time that I was taking a Biblical Research Methods class for my doctorate, my brother Dan MacInnis was being promoted to Rear Admiral of the US Navy. He asked me to Pray the invocation prayer at his pinning ceremony.

The Lord had me research Daniel in the Bible and pull out everything that I could from his life that was relevant to leadership. After thorough research, the Lord gave Dan this journal message which summarized the key points learned in the research. These points were woven into the invocation prayer as well. Here is what the Lord gave to Dan.

You are named after one of the great leaders of the Bible. Daniel was able to see and hear my voice. He was faithful and courageous in the face of danger. Daniel worked under tyrannical kings and earned their respect. He succeeded in everything that He did by My power and might. Daniel's life as he served under the four kings, exemplifies the key principles of the great leader reinforced in the Scriptures that Patty has researched. He was a servant leader. I would like for you to remember these important things as you lead:

1. *When you serve with a pure heart and selfless pure motives, I AM pleased.*
2. *Once you prove that you are trustworthy, I promote you and give you more responsibility, just as I am doing for you now with this new role.*
3. *I will always give you an increased anointing, that is My power through the Holy Spirit, to do what I'm calling you to do.*
4. *I will always reward your faithful service.*
5. *As I give you more responsibility, so I grow my expectations for you to serve with humility, integrity, and honor. When much is given, much is required.*

Dearest *Dan,*

Don't get caught up in the busyness of your job as if what you do makes you important. It's not what you do that matters most, it's who you are and who you are becoming that is the most important thing. To be successful in what you do, you must first be successful in who you are. Humility precedes honor. Meditation on the Scriptures precedes wisdom. And success in small things leads to greater responsibilities and greater successes.

When you learn to keep your eyes fixed on Me, Jesus, the Author, and Finisher of your faith, then you will be transformed into the very best version of yourself. You will find that you will be more successful with less effort. When you learn to trust Me with every aspect of your life, then I will be able to trust you with greater and greater responsibilities. Be still, let go, see striving, relax, and know that I AM God. (Psalm 46:10)

Walk with Me. See My will, and you and I will do amazing things together! I am trusting you with this new opportunity and important responsibility. Now trust ME! I AM God. Believe it and be satisfied!

With everlasting love,

Jesus

When Dan retired from the Navy after his season as Admiral was completed, our family attended his retirement ceremony. We had no idea when we got there, that the formal military ball that he had invited us to was in his honor. We were seated at the head table and people shared stories of their connections with him as a leader. I was never more proud of him than I was at that moment. He left a mark that truly reflected what Jesus had called him to be and do in that journal entry.

My First Destiny Cave Encounter

One day, I asked Jesus to take me somewhere new. We walked from my special place through a path in the woods lined with vibrant flowers that opened to a stunning river and a great tree at its bank. The flowers were alive, and as Jesus passed, the flowers sang His praises. The river was flowing with colors, like the rare ones in the ultimate crayon collection, and others I don't think I have ever seen before. The colors were all independently flowing together but not mixing themselves up.

Some were subtle and others demanded notice. The water was crystal clear. Not like heavy paint flowing, but fresh, crisp, colorful water.

Then we climbed up a huge mountain and walked through a path inside the mountain. There were dozens of cave tunnel options. Jesus knew exactly where He was going, and I followed. We finished our journey by walking into a round cave room with high stone walls and one large table that seemed to be made from the trunk of a long-based tree. It reminded me of a large petrified wood sample that I saw in the Petrified Forest National Park in Arizona. There was a stone-platformed balcony and Jesus took me out there.

There was a beautifully colored waterfall to the left and the River below. There were cave balconies cut into the miles-high gorge of the River of Living Water. Walking back inside, Jesus said.

> *This is your Destiny Cave. It holds your past, present, and future possibilities that are written in the Book of your life's destiny.*

Jesus and I walked up to the long table. There is a carved line down the center and other lines coming off the main one, with others coming off them. In my vision, it looked something like this with many more veins.

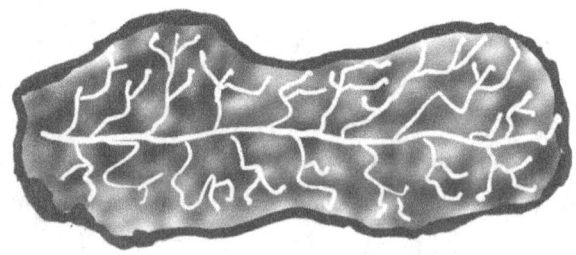

This is your destiny map. Touch it.

When I touched the left side of the table moving pictures of my childhood filled the walls of my cave all the way around. They were memories of things in my life. When I touched farther up to the right, the walls filled up with scenes of things that had not happened yet. I saw a much older me with all gray hair speaking on a platform with an untold number of people. There were other scenes of people reading my books and healing miracles.

> *Those are scenes of the plans I have for you should you stay aligned to My will. It is a picture of the Jeremiah 29:11 plans I have for you. See what I have for you when you humble yourself and seek and cooperate with what I want to do through you?*

Yes, Lord, it's amazing!

> *I need you to carry the Good News to the people I have for you to influence.*

He took me by the shoulders and looked right into my eyes and said.

> *Thank you for your willingness to serve for My sake and my sheep. Thank you for stewarding the gifts, talents, and skills that I have developed in you for your unique purpose. Through challenges and trials, you didn't give up. Continue to remain faithful to Me for each assignment I give you and you will see these future glimpses come to pass. I am prepared to release unprecedented favor in this season for those who are willing to serve with a pure heart.*

> *What looks impossible or does not make sense in the natural will come to pass by my empowering Holy Spirit. Your testimony will be; not by my might, nor by my power, but by God's Spirit it was accomplished!*

Amen! Yes. Lord!

Encountering the Waymaker

Your Favorite Parts of Me

- Meet the Waymaker in your Special Place as a child and play with Him for a bit.

- Ask Him to show you His favorite things about you that He created specifically for your Kingdom Purpose. They could be characteristics, skills, talents, or even heart motivations.

- Then let Him show you a glimpse of you serving using them in the future.

Seeing the Waymaker Past

- Meet the Waymaker in your Special place as a child.

- Ask Him to take you to your Destiny Room, explore this space and ask Him anything you need to understand.

- Ask Him to take you to a memory of a moment in time where you would consider a turning point in your life. It was a time when your interests, aptitudes, or talents were recognized.

- Talk to Him about how He has nurtured and developed those things to prepare you for your calling and destiny.

- What insights do you have about your present and future because of your past?

Me in the Big Kingdom Plan

- Meet the Waymaker either in your Destiny Room or in your Special Place. Spend time just being with Him for a few minutes.

- Ask Him to reveal to you either the people or types of people for which He is linking you in your Kingdom purposes. What part are you offering? What parts are you needing others to play? Ask Him to show you the Kingdom impact that is there for you if you live a life totally aligned with Him.

Help Me Find it by Sidewalk Prophets

https://youtu.be/CsjZ94K7UQs

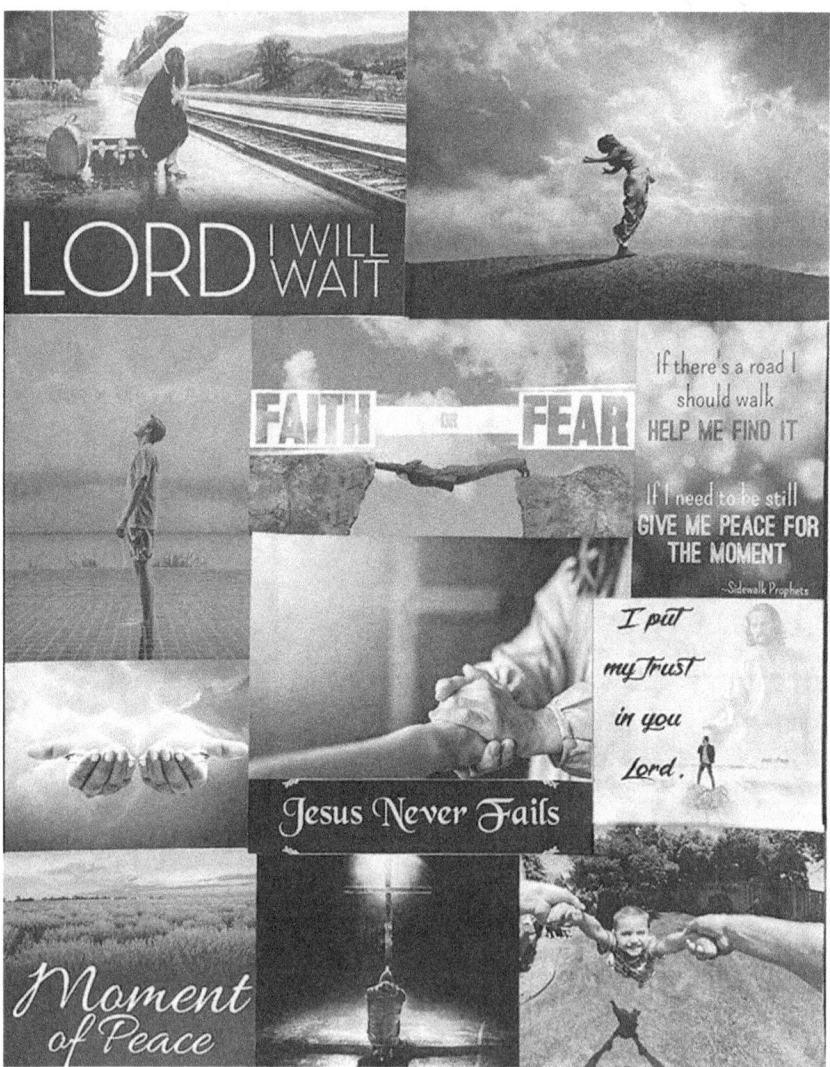

Meet the Supernatural Provider

O f the Hebrew Names of God commonly used in Christian circles, Jehovah Jireh is at the top of the list. The name means *the LORD will provide.* Yet, many who think they know this Name have a limited understanding of it.

Jehovah Jireh is a compound name. Jehovah is one of the Names that include the fullness of all that God is, was, and always will be. It encapsulates God's full nature, character, and will. The Lord explained the name Jehovah to me as the fullness of His "Is-ness". It is everything that He is apart from us for which we are not a factor.

Jireh means provider. This word describes something that God does. It is a "Does-ness" Name of God. When Jehovah Jireh shows up, His provision is always supernatural. Remember, when you add the fullness of God to His provision, He brings the resources from heaven to bear. Yet, most people pray limited natural realm prayers. God has so much more for you than you think.

Abraham gave God this name in Genesis chapter 22 as a demonstration of his faithful expectation that the LORD would provide a lamb. This was the nature of his test when he was asked to sacrifice his son Isaac and the Lord stayed his hand.

Genesis 22:7-8 [7] And Isaac said to Abraham, "My father!" And he said, "Here I am, my son." Isaac said, "Look, the fire and the wood, but where is the lamb for the burnt offering?" [8] Abraham said, "My son, God will provide for Himself [f]a lamb for the burnt offering." So the two walked on together.

The word for provide above is *raah*[23] which means; to see, appeared, displayed, give attention, enjoy, face, make me see, looking, observing, perceiving, view or watch, keep looking, to see plainly, to give understanding, watching, provision. This is an interesting list. Did you notice that it was mostly about your eyes?

Abraham passed this test because he remembered the promise the Lord gave him that the descendants of Isaac would number the grains of sand on the seashore and stars of the sea.

Hebrews 11:17-19 [17] By faith Abraham, when he was tested [that is, as the testing of his faith was still in progress], [a] offered up Isaac, and he who had received the promises [of God] was ready to sacrifice his only son [of promise]; [18] to whom it was said, "THROUGH ISAAC YOUR DESCENDANTS SHALL BE CALLED." [19] For he considered [it reasonable to believe] that God was able to raise *Isaac* even from among the dead. [Indeed, in the sense that he was prepared to sacrifice Isaac in obedience to God] Abraham did receive him back [from the dead] figuratively speaking.

Genesis 22:12-14 [12] The LORD said, "Do not reach out [with the knife in] your hand against the boy, and do nothing to [harm] him; for now I know that you fear God [with reverence and profound respect], since you have not withheld from Me your son, your only son [of promise]." [13] Then Abraham looked up and glanced around, and behold, behind him was a ram caught in a thicket by his horns. And Abraham went and took the ram and offered it up for a burnt offering (ascending sacrifice) instead of his son. [14] So

---

[23] https://biblehub.com/hebrew/7200.htm search lexicon for Genesis 22:14 word 'provide' = raah.

Abraham named that place [a]The LORD Will Provide. And it is said to this day, "On the mountain of the LORD it [b]will be seen *and* provided."

The Lord said because you have obeyed, (*shamata* which means; listened obediently, pay attention, listen, heard for certain, heeded, proclaimed and understood, witnessed to) My voice about the promise, you have proved your faith that you actively believe and you don't need to kill your son. God was pointing out the conditions that were met: Abraham heard, saw, and obeyed God.

Abraham heard God's voice, he looked and found the ram stuck in the thickets, and he obeyed God's direction. Then he named the place God will provide. You must see and listen and obey God's direction for the Lord to provide supernaturally. These are the minimum requirements for this promise.

The Observer Effect

There is a fascinating scientific discovery in quantum physics that when you look at something, it changes. Scientists call this the Observer Effect. In 1998, Weizmann Institute researchers were studying how electrons behaved at the submicron level.

Science Snippet: The Observer Effect[24]
https://youtu.be/ShqXYRWqvWA

---

[24] Science Snippet: The Observer Effect by Jen Foxbit https://youtu.be/ShqXYRWqvWA

A machine shot photons (light atoms) through a slit in a metal panel to a back surface to see the patterns of how they hit it. As the atoms hit the wall, they revealed dots that formed the shape of the slit.

When they tried it with two slits in the metal panel, they saw two columns of dots. They concluded that photons behaved like particles. They wanted to understand this more, so they used a microscopic viewing machine that could see this activity at the atomic level to observe and measure them with microscopic accuracy.

This machine was set up like a microscopic eyeball to observe carefully and slowly the behavior of the photons up close. The strangest thing happened when they did that. The photons started to behave like waves instead of particles.

Waves roll creating ripples and because the atoms were waving through the slits, they began bumping into each other, so it was no longer two lines but patterns that looked like waves. The only change in the control of this experiment was observation. The scientists concluded that looking at something changes it. As they looked at the data they watched the atoms flatten and transform.

> Hebrews 2:1-2 Therefore, since we are surrounded by so great a cloud of [a]witnesses [who by faith have testified to the truth of God's absolute faithfulness], stripping off every unnecessary weight and the sin which so easily *and* cleverly entangles us, let us run with endurance *and* active persistence the race that is set before us, [2] [looking away from all that will distract us and] focusing our eyes on Jesus, who is the Author and Perfecter of faith [the first incentive for our belief and the One who brings our faith to maturity], who for the joy [of accomplishing the

goal] set before Him endured the cross, [b]disregarding the shame, and sat down at the right hand of the throne of God [revealing His deity, His authority, and the completion of His work].

Fix your eyes on Jesus. When you look at Him you are transformed. Your perspective shifts from looking at the natural world and circumstances to looking at Him. This causes you to see through His eyes, feel with His heart, and think His thoughts. When you look at Him your perspective changes.

When you look at Jesus, He feels your focus on Him and He looks back at you. When He looks at you, He is transformed. That is, He becomes motivated to act on your behalf. In Encountering the HEALING of God: Experience Jesus Book 2, we learned that when you picture Jesus and agree with His truth, your body begins to agree with that truth at the cellular level and heals your body. The observer effect is the science that backs that up!

Encounters with God are not just figments of your imagination. They powerfully transform you!

Hearing and Speaking

Seeing AND hearing are both involved in the transformation and both are important.

> Romans 10:17 [17] So faith *comes* from hearing [what is told], and what is heard *comes* by the [preaching of the] message concerning Christ.

Sounds are vibrations. I asked the Lord about seeing and hearing and He said.

I need you to do your part. That is, stay close to Me so you can speak in agreement with what I am saying and doing. In this way, you will learn how to be fully equipped to live and serve out of the full anointing of the Holy Spirit. Then, when you are able, you will help others to do the same. Together we will create a mighty wave that can rock the very foundation of the earth.

What we do together creates a wave and ripples out and affects other people. When spirit anointed people pray out loud in agreement with My will, they activate My power, and nothing can stop My will and Kingdom plan.

Isaiah 55:10 [10] "For as the rain and snow come down from heaven, And do not return there without watering the earth, making it bear and sprout, And providing seed to the sower and bread to the eater, [11] So will My word be which goes out of My mouth; It will not return to Me void (useless, without result), Without accomplishing what I desire, And without succeeding *in the matter* for which I sent it.

That's one of the reasons I think we need to speak God's word and promises out loud. Because when we speak out loud, we release the creation vibrations of God's will to accomplish His purposes in this natural realm.

Horton Hears a Who Clips

In this Dr. Seuss classic, Horton is a big elephant in a big world and the Whos are tiny beings whose world is a spec to Horton. The little people need to believe the voice first. He warns them and tries to get his world to believe that the little world of people exists. Jesus directed me to these two film clips as illustrations of an important truth.

We are Here Clip1[25]

https://youtu.be/MoOwbXap6LM

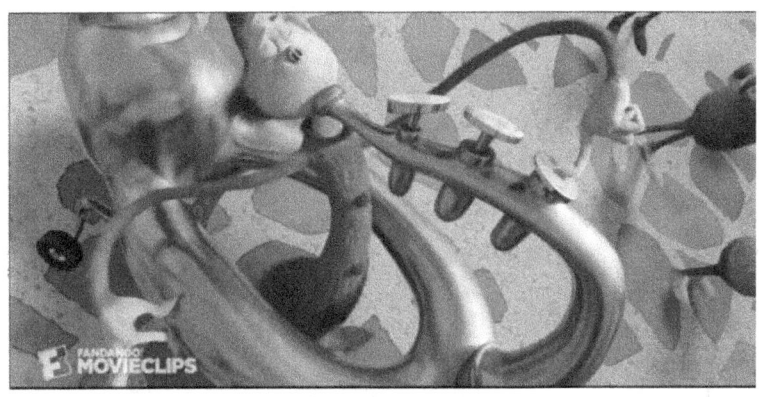

JoJo Saves the Day[26]

https://youtu.be/mur1iXhfJ5E

This is what Jesus had to say about these film clips:

This is My heart for the nations and the world. It's like Horton Hears a Who. When the small people on the speck believed

---

[25] We are Here clip from Horton Hears a Who by Dr. Suess, film by Blue Sky Studios https://youtu.be/MoOwbXap6LM

26 JoJo Saves the Day clip from Horton Hears a Who by Dr. Suess, film by Blue Sky Studios https://youtu.be/mur1iXhfJ5E

the voice, they came together and made their voices heard. When you do the same, I will magnify, multiply, and act powerfully in your favor. Be persistent, faithful, and relentless in your hunger and thirst for Me, My time and My plan. Stay connected to the vine so you can produce healthy fruit for My kingdom purposes.

Provisional Guidance and Lessons of Radical Obedience

This is the story of Kris Castro's approximately 14,000-mile journey over about six months, guided one step and day at a time by the Lord's direction.

Kris Castro and I were long-distance acquaintances about 8 years before this story began. I knew her as an online colleague when we belonged to the same website platform marketing community. We were connected on LinkedIn and Facebook, but we were not close friends.

I received a phone call from her asking if she could come to Cleveland and spend two nights at my house. I'm not sure why it was so easy to say yes to that request other than I sensed it was God's idea. George and I welcomed her into our house.

It all started with a prophetic message. Below is Kris' record of it.

6/6/18 A prophetic word from Mary Held (about a month before He invited me on the Adventure) – "I'm underneath a glass floor. I see you walking and then you stop, and then you walk again. As you were walking you were looking down because you can't see the floor. The Lord said you are going to have seasons in this transition of life, and you will go on a journey where you step without being sure there's something to step on here...but you're going to do it. I just encourage you that He is your floor. It may appear there's no floor to step out on, but your faith will take you there."

This is Kris sharing her testimony of what happened beginning one month after that prophetic message.

Kris Castro Testimony of Radical Obedience

http://begintoshift.com/crazy-adventure-book/

Kris knew God wanted her in Cleveland and didn't know of any Celebrate Recovery people in the area to contact. God brought me to mind, and she contacted me. I was not connected in any way that I knew of with Celebrate Recovery. But when Kris visited us, she attended my Spirit Life Circle and one of the ladies in that group knew who used to lead those meetings. Oddly, that person was a friend of mine in college who I hadn't talked with in a long time. But I still had his phone number. We were able to connect with him the next day. Coincidence? There is no such thing with God!"

I called Kris and interviewed her so I could include her reflections about her journey now more than four years past the experience. I asked her to share some of her learnings from the adventure. Here are the highlights of what she said.

"The Lord is really who He says He is, and you can only really know that experientially. I had never experienced His goodness, protection, faithfulness provision, and direction so fully and personally before this adventure. I came back knowing who He IS. God has brought me so far now. I have developed a lifestyle of cliff jumping with the Lord. If He could pull me through that, I can jump off any cliff for Him. I know He's got me! Through this crazy road trip journey, I have truly learned what radical obedience looks like. I understand experientially the peace that surpasses understanding. And learned the power of a mighty story." ~ Kris Castro

She had a real beater of a car. My husband George was concerned that she would not make it across the country in that car, so he serviced it for her while she was with us. It made it to Washington state before breaking down and needing a 5-day repair. This was an opportunity for the Lord to show her His mighty provision by providing the additional housing and the full repair costs!

Kris recorded her adventure in a Vlog and made it a practice of taking a photo with each host family that took her in. Here is the picture of her with George and me.

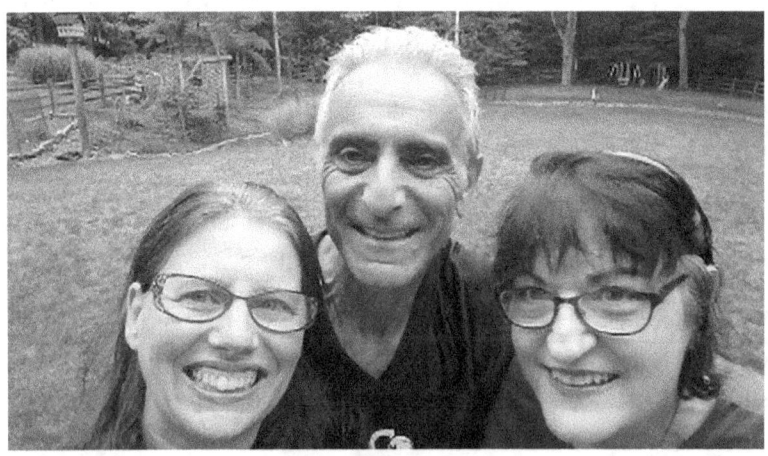

Today Kris' ministry is all about helping people tell their stories to advance Kingdom purposes. For more information about her journey and ministry, check out her book, *"Crazy" Might be a Blessing in Disguise,* and visit her website at https://begintoshift.com/.

Bible Stories of Miraculous Provision

The Bible is replete with stories of God's miraculous provision.

> 2 Kings 4:1-7 ¹ Now one of the wives *of a man* of the [a] sons of the prophets cried out to Elisha [for help], saying "Your servant my husband is dead, and you know that your servant [reverently] feared the LORD; but the creditor is coming to take my two sons to be his slaves [in payment for a loan]." ² Elisha said to her, "What shall I do for you? Tell me, what do you have [of value] in the house?" She said, "Your maidservant has nothing in the house except a [small] jar of [olive] oil." ³ Then he said, "Go, borrow containers from all your neighbors, empty containers—and not *just* a few. ⁴ Then you shall go in and shut the door behind you and your sons, and pour out [the oil you have] into all these containers, and you shall set aside each one when it is full." ⁵ So she left him and shut the door behind her and her sons; they were bringing her *the containers* as she poured [the oil]. ⁶ When the containers were all full, she said to her son, "Bring me another container." And he said to her, "There is not a one left." Then the oil stopped [multiplying]. ⁷ Then she came and told the man of God. He said, "Go, sell the oil and pay your debt, and you and your sons can live on the rest."

This woman obeyed the request that seemed illogical. She offered *what she had* and God multiplied it. She offered faith, obedience, and a small amount of oil. That faithful act of obedience was what it took for the Supernatural Provider to show up and supply enough to pay off her debts and keep her and her sons alive through the season of famine and lack.

Among other wonderous Biblical stories, there is the miracle of God feeding the Israelites manna. (See Exodus 16) They referred to manna as the bread of heaven because it fell from the sky six days a week and fed the Israelites for 40 years. It was just enough for each day. If they tried to save it, it would turn rotten the next day.

The manna did not fall on the Sabbath, because they were not allowed to work on Sabbath. So, the day before the Sabbath, a double portion would fall and remain good for two days. This was a sign of the Lord supernaturally caring for the physical needs of His people.

Jesus referred to Himself as the *Bread of Life.*

> John 6:35 [35] Jesus replied to them, "[a]I am the Bread of Life. The one who comes to Me will never be hungry, and the one who believes in Me [as Savior] will never be thirsty [for that one will be sustained spiritually].

God provided manna to sustain the Israelites in the wilderness physically and He sent Jesus to provide spiritual food for our needs.

God's Financial Provision

Jeanette and her husband Denny had twins about to graduate from High School and head off to college. They had a third child who would be graduating only two years after her brothers. So, there would be a season with three in college. Jeanette will take the story from here by sharing her testimony.

> "Spencer was a stellar student, actively involved in school and sports, and graduated in the top 10 of his class. In

addition, he was very focused on wanting to earn a degree in engineering, thus narrowing his choice of colleges to attend upon graduation from high school. It seemed like this should be an easy decision of where to attend and that some financial assistance could be obtained. Boy, were we wrong!"

"After being tossed around by his first-choice college, we eventually received word that he was not accepted. We were at a complete loss. None of the other schools were offering him money, other than loans, and we didn't know what to do, or where to go. Then one day while my husband and I were talking about it with Spencer, the Lord spoke in His ever so gentle voice and said to me;

"Have you asked Spencer the DESIRE of HIS heart? Because I put it there!"

"Immediately, I halted our conversation and asked Spencer if he could go anywhere, regardless of money, what would that desire be. He answered the "University of Cincinnati". Knowing that it was about $25,000 per year and that despite all Spencer's diligent efforts during high school he didn't receive one dime in assistance, we weren't sure how we were going to pay for it. Sure, loans were available but as Denny says, "loans don't aid. They're a burden." So, we were hurt. In Spencer's words "what else could I have done?" With tear-filled eyes, we had no answer. So, I looked up to God and said, "You need to figure this out.".

"And sure enough, the Lord did figure it out! Just not in the way we would have preferred. His plan was for Denny to lose his job! Yes, two weeks after Spencer's decision, and with two boys set to attend college in the fall, our main source of income was swept away. And no unemployment was received. And with that, we contacted the financial aid office hoping to receive a small amount of aid. All summer long, nothing different happened. No word on any aid and we just assumed that it didn't matter. Less than a week before tuition was due, we received a notice that our financial aid status changed. We had no idea what that meant and upon calling the university, they had no idea either. Not seeing or hearing anything, we nearly drained an account and paid the tuition bill the day before it was due."

"Then as God would have it, after the act of obedience of us paying the bill, God paid us. We received a credit in our account the very day tuition was due. And not just for one semester, but for two. The amount was five times as much as we were even hoping for! Only God!"

"We learned a valuable lesson. God's ways are indeed higher than ours. Since then, we have continued to be blessed. The program Spencer is enrolled in is designed to include several paid co-ops that are required for a degree. Thus, Spencer can work and earn money one semester, and then pay for the next. God knew all along how we were going to be able to afford this. And I should note that Spencer's first school of choice does not have such a program. What a blessing that he didn't get accepted into that school as he would have had to take out a large loan for sure. Praise God!!! He knew the better path for us."

"P.S. We also experienced many other financial blessings during the 10 weeks that Denny was unemployed. True miracles! God showed us He is our Provider, and since then, we have never worried about provision. God is our source!"
~ Jeanette Chamberlin

God's ways are different than ours, so we need to remember to never tell HIM how He's supposed to meet our needs. And not to pray below God's best. Just enough to meet your natural situation is not God's plan for you! Pray God's BEST. You don't need to know what that means, just trust that He knows what that means.

The Principle of Sowing and Reaping

Sowing and reaping is a supernatural law. We understand and respect the law of gravity. This Spiritual principle is no less of a law. It doesn't just apply to provision or money as many think. It works for everything: your words, heart posture, and actions.

What you sow, you reap. Everything is a seed. A seed is the design of a thing. A tree does not bear a different fruit than its seed. Seeds hold the capability of future outcomes according to their design. If you are a person who speaks negativity, with words of lack or hopelessness, then you will reap those things. Saying things like: I will never lose weight, or I will always live paycheck to paycheck, will cause those seeds to be planted in your heart and mind, and they will bear that fruit.

We will learn more about this principle in the Meet the Creator chapter of *How to Encounter the POWER of God: Experience Jesus Book 4* about how God created everything in the universe with His words and we are created in His image. Your sown words create and reap your future realities.

Be careful how you use your words. Do you speak hope or hopelessness, health or sickness, forgiveness or unforgiveness? Your words set into motion those realities.

Just like in gardening, there is a cycle. You sow a seed, and then there is a waiting season while you care for the plant, and then it is ready to reap a harvest. The same is true with the spiritual law of sowing and reaping. When you sow consistently, you are always reaping because you are always sowing. And even though you are still waiting for the seed to bear fruit, each seed reaches fruit-bearing in its turn. So, a lifestyle of steady sowing will reap a continuous harvest. Many people give sporadically and wonder why they are in financial trouble.

More important than consistency is your heart posture. God speaks the language of the heart and knows your true motivation. Sow grudgingly, and it doesn't count as positive sowing, but as negative sowing. Because what you are sowing is resentment or stinginess. Sowing with a heart of gratitude is the kind that reaps great blessings.

With the proper heart posture, you know that all you have is God's anyway, so giving 10% is the minimum you will want to give when your heart wants it used for God's glory. This kind of giving brings you joy.

To be a receiver of multiplied plenty from the Lord, you must be a gracious giver. The first time I was at Bethel in Cleveland, a pastor at the pulpit said, "It's offering time, " and folks were cheering! I looked around in confusion about that! But I learned what they already knew, giving with a heart of gratitude returns 10,30,50 or 100-fold as the scriptures promise.

We learn in Matthew chapter 13, in the parable of the soils that good soil is required for multiplied blessings.

> Matthew 13:8 Other seed fell on good soil and yielded grain, some a hundred times as much [as was sown], some sixty [times as much], and some thirty.

This is God's way, and it is revealed in nature. There are five seeds in every apple. One seed can produce an apple tree with an average of 120 apples. God is a God of multiplication. And not just simple multiplication, it's X factor multiplication. Knowing this important principle, it makes sense to speak a prayer over each tithe and offering. Tell Him your heart for how He may multiply it.

This brings me back to our definition of the provision of God being connected to seeing with the eyes of your heart what the Lord is doing, so you agree with Him. Pay attention because He multiplies in ways you may not connect to your sowing in the natural. You can see that truth in Jeanette's story!

Since the Lord challenges us to taste and see that the Lord is good, (Psalm 34:8) Test God in this principle of sowing and reaping. For one month, give more than you think you can with the proper heart of gratitude, desire to bless and honor God and watch what He will do with that.

There is power in thankfulness. Blessings flow to a person with a grateful heart.

The Lord took me to a stream in my spirit one day. He asked me to make a tight fist and dip my hands in the water.

He asked me, *"How much water can a fist hold on to?*

"None, Lord," I answered.

"This is the heart posture of a stingy person. Now cup your hands."

Then Jesus poured water into my cupped hands, and some remained in my hands while the rest of it poured into the stream. The stream grew bigger until it became a mighty river.

> Jesus explained, *"What is in your hands is what you need. The rest is there to pass through your hands to bless others. Allow Me to flow blessing to and through you by opening your heart and hands to My provisional blessings."*

> John 10:10 The thief comes only in order to steal and kill and destroy. I came that they may have and enjoy life, and have it in abundance [to the full, till it overflows].

God is not against prosperity as some would claim. He is against selfishness. God delights in blessing the ones who have no selfish motives. It is one of the reasons He came. Abraham, David, Solomon, and Job were counted as God's favorite people, and they were all wealthy. God prospered them to be wealthy.

So how do reconcile that reality with the verse,

> Matthew 19:24 Again I tell you, it is easier for a camel to go through the eye of a needle, than for a rich man [who places his faith in wealth and status] to enter the kingdom of God.

The key difference is the heart posture. Is the person selfish, or selfless? People often misquote the word by saying that money is the root of all evil. But the word actually says that the *love* of money is the root of all evil. That is the heart posture of someone worshipping money over God. The difference is 100 % about your heart posture.

> 1 Timothy 6:10 For the love of money [that is, the greedy desire for it and the willingness to gain it unethically] is a root of all sorts of evil, and some by longing for it have wandered away from the faith and pierced themselves [through and through] with many sorrows.

The parable of the talents shared in Matthew chapter 25 teaches you that if you can be trusted with little, God will trust you with more. The parable shares about giving three men money and asking them to steward it. While two of the men multiplied what was given, the third man dug a hole in the ground and hid it, then returned it. The Master in the parable rebuked the man who hid the talent in the ground and did not multiply it, calling him wicked. All gifts from God are there to be used for God's glory and intended to be multiplied.

Selfishness blocks Gods provision. Humility opens the floodgates of heavenly resources on your behalf. Be careful to not push away God's blessings without even realizing it, because of the lie of unworthiness. You are a child of the living God, and He makes you worthy. Jesus found you worthy enough to die for, so don't nullify that sacrifice by a sense of unworthiness. When someone offers to pay for your lunch, or do you a favor, do you politely refuse? Perhaps you are robbing that person of a sowed blessing. Don't push away God's blessings.

> 2 Corinthians 9:6-9 ⁶ Now [remember] this: he who sows sparingly will also reap sparingly, and he who sows [a] generously [that blessings may come to others] will also reap [b]generously [and be blessed]. ⁷ Let each one give [thoughtfully and with purpose] just as he has decided in his heart, not grudgingly or under compulsion, for God loves a cheerful giver [and delights in the one whose heart is in his gift]. ⁸ And God is able to make all grace [every favor and earthly blessing] come in abundance to you, so that you may always [under all circumstances, regardless of the need] have complete sufficiency in everything [being completely self-sufficient in Him], and have an abundance for every good work and act of charity. ⁹ As it is written and forever remains written.

A seed not sown does not multiply!

Provisional Equipping

How does God do it? What is His Process?

> Ephesians 3:16-19 ¹⁶ May He grant you out of the riches of His glory, to be strengthened *and* spiritually energized with power through His Spirit in your inner self, [indwelling your innermost being and personality], ¹⁷ so that Christ may dwell in your hearts through your faith. And may

you, having been [deeply] rooted and [securely] grounded in love, [18] be fully capable of comprehending with all the saints (God's people) the width and length and height and depth of His love [fully experiencing that amazing, endless love]; [19] and [that you may come] to know [practically, through personal experience] the love of Christ which far surpasses [mere] knowledge [without experience], that you may be filled up [throughout your being] to all the fullness of God [so that you may have the richest experience of God's presence in your lives, completely filled and flooded with God Himself].

The Senses of the Heart and Cycles of Behavior

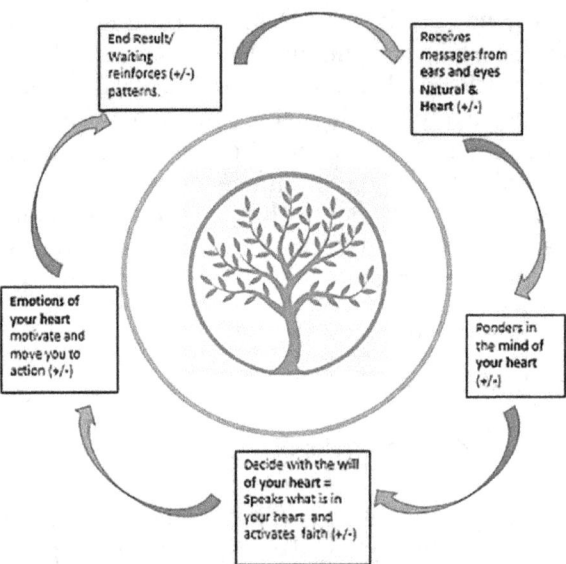

The Senses of the Heart and Cycles of Behavior

Just as the body has five senses; seeing, hearing, smelling, touching, and tasting, so the inner man, or heart has five senses as well. These spiritual senses are the eyes, ears, mind, will and emotions of the heart. The heart is the container for our spirits and when you are saved, it houses the Holy Spirit as well. The Holy Spirit uses these inner man senses to communicate and guide you throughout your life.

Knowing about these senses is an important first step to being able to understand yourself and others. The model above works in both the positive and the negative. When it is working in the negative, your starting point is worldly; when it is working in the positive, the starting point is Jesus, empowered by the Holy Spirit.

Let's look at this model to see how a reinforcing pattern works in both the negative and the positive. The circle represents your heart. Begin with receiving messages from your eyes and ears. Notice that you receive messages from both your natural senses perceiving the physical world, and your spiritual eyes and ears of your heart.

Notice the arrows. One step leads you to the next, with reinforcing momentum. If you begin by receiving positive information with your eye/ear senses, it moves you in a positive direction. If you begin with negative information, you move clockwise around the circle, but your outcome will be negative.

Here we learn that the Holy Spirit comes in fullness and brings the capability to access the very mind of Christ so that we may be transformed into our ideal Christ identity.

You receive messages from the Lord using the eyes and ears of your heart. Seeing and hearing from God with the eyes and ears of your heart allows you to see His vision and hear His voice. To discern its meaning, you ponder what you have received with your inner mind by tapping into God's wisdom to understand it. Faith rises and doubts are removed when you receive God's clarity and wisdom.

When you agree with His will, you purpose in your spirit to obey it which causes you to speak in faith activating the intention to obey what He says. The act of speaking mobilizes your faith and germinates the seed in your heart. This alignment with your heart to God connects you with His emotion and fuels your faith to act in agreement with God's will. This cooperation with God's mind, will, and emotion produces the manifestation of His miraculous promises in your life.

How you handle the waiting season is another test of faith. Will you continue to stand on the promises of God? Or will you allow fears and anxieties to trigger faith in reverse?

It all begins with where your eyes are fixed. Will you choose to fix your eyes on God's truth? Or on the world's limitations?

Baptism of the Holy Spirit

When the Holy Spirit comes to dwell in the heart of a believer, He comes in whole, not in part. The *capability* of all nine manifestation gifts is in the hearts of believers. The release of those gifts is at the discretion of the Holy Spirit. This is what is meant by "to one is given..." which implies the circumstance for releasing the gift, not as a gift itself. (See 1 Corinthians 12:7-10)

The gifts are given when you are saved and then activated by the baptism of the Holy Spirit. At the point of salvation when you accept Jesus as your Savior, there is a seed deposited in your heart that contains the design and capability of the fullness of the Holy Spirit. The time of salvation justifies your eternal destination of heaven. But just like any seed, it's not meant to remain a seed. Seeds have the design within them to become fruit-bearing plants.

The baptism of the Holy Spirit waters that seed in fertile soil and begins the process of growing you into that powerful fruit-bearing vessel that God sees you as already. The Holy Spirit baptism is both about living water and God's fire. God's fire does not destroy but refines, burning off anything that hinders you from becoming who He has created you to be and to do. The fire leads to humility and repentance. These two characteristics are necessary for the Holy Spirit to move in your heart and life.

Unlike your salvation baptism, which justifies and seals you for eternity, the baptism of the Holy Spirit is for sanctification which is your continued growth in Christ. Once baptized in the Spirit you still need constant refilling. Even though you have been filled with the Holy Spirit, you can lose your way and get caught up in the world, busyness, and other life circumstances and leave the Holy Spirit dormant in your heart. Holy habits of seeking God's face not His hand and remaining hungry for God's presence, keep your spiritual tank filled up.

1Corinthians 12:31 But earnestly desire and strive for the greater gifts. And yet I will show you a still more excellent way [one of the choicest graces and the highest of them all: unselfish love].

So, before we even dive into the nine manifestation gifts, here is an opportunity for you to pray to ask for the baptism of the Holy Spirit. Repeat this prayer out loud with a sincere heart.

Heavenly Father,

You promised in Acts 1:5-8 that Your disciples would receive power and ability when the Holy Spirit would come upon us. You promised to give us the power to be Your witnesses even to the ends of the earth in Acts chapter 2.

Holy Spirit, come upon me now in your fullness. I yield myself to You. I receive by faith the baptism of the Holy Spirit. I welcome you, Holy Spirit, in the Name of Jesus. Thank You for empowering me for Your service.

Fill me with boldness and courage to speak Your Word with power. I receive this wonderful empowerment by faith. As promised in John 14:26, send me the Holy Spirit, the Advocate, to teach me all things and remind me of everything You teach in Your Word. Give me a contagious hunger for your Presence Lord, so I may be filled to overflowing and release your love and light in the world. I desire spiritual gifts according to Your Word and ask You to grant me Your spiritual giftings according to Your will for my life. I joyfully accept Your gifts for me. Thank you for all that you are and all that I am in YOU, in Jesus' Name. amen.

The Manifestation Gifts of the Holy Spirit

The Lord described the Holy Spirit manifestation gifts as hidden behind closed but unlocked doors in your heart. Technically we all have the ability for any of the gifts to be released, but it is the Holy Spirit who decides that you are ready to release a gift.

> Ephesians 4:7 ⁷ Yet grace was given to each one of us [not indiscriminately, but in different ways] in proportion to the measure of Christ's [rich and abundant] gift.

Even the level at which you release these gifts can grow as you grow in maturity. Gifts are released according to your ability to handle them. He won't give you more than your maturity level or you might take pride in the gifts. God cannot come near pride.

> James 4:6 ⁶ But He gives us more and more grace [through the power of the Holy Spirit to defy sin and live an obedient life that reflects both our faith and our gratitude for our

176

salvation]. Therefore, it says, "GOD IS OPPOSED TO THE PROUD *and* HAUGHTY, BUT [continually] GIVES [the gift of] GRACE TO THE HUMBLE [who turn away from self-righteousness]."

The word 'oppose' in the Bible is *antitassó* which means to range in battle against, to set oneself against, to resist, to actively fight against! God will certainly not empower someone acting haughty or proud with the gifts of the Spirit!

So, the gifts are released according to your faith level and your spiritual maturity. When you agree with God and are humble and open to being serviceable for His Kingdom purposes, these gifts will be released in you.

Obedience to the promptings of the Holy Spirit is important to prove your readiness. If you can receive a word of knowledge but lack the courage when God asks you to share it as a prophecy, He will not trust you for more when you don't obey Him with it. The secret to obedience is realizing that it is not you, but Christ in you that is releasing the gifts. All you are doing is being the willing vessel to release it.

Think of it as working a job and the boss sees that you are ready for more responsibility. The boss is the one that gives you that upgraded assignment or promotion. When the Holy Spirit finds you mature enough to handle a gift and ready to be trusted to release it for His purposes, He will open the doors.

God inspires us uniquely by our talents as well. He intertwines these manifestation gifts uniquely in cooperation with your skills and talents.

Exodus 28:3 ³ Tell all the skilled *and* talented people whom I have endowed with a spirit of wisdom, that they are to make Aaron's garments to sanctify him *and* set him apart to serve as a priest for Me.

Everything God does is motivated by love. So, everything He will give you to do must also be motivated by Love.

> 1 Corinthians 13:2 [2] And if I have *the gift of* prophecy [and speak a new message from God to the people], and understand all mysteries, and [possess] all knowledge; and if I have all [sufficient] faith so that I can remove mountains, but do not have love [reaching out to others], I am nothing.

When we shift off that central focus, take pride in the gifting, or take credit for God's glory, He will stop using us. Gifts are given according to God's grace. Use your gift according to the grace given to you. Know your lane. Don't go above your authority and use a gift apart from the Holy Spirit's instruction.

Three Categories of Manifestation Gifts.

I find it easier to remember the manifestation gifts if I divide them into mind, mouth, and hand gifts. Some call the mind one's *revelational gifts,* the mouth one's *vocal gifts,* and the hand one's the *power gifts.* So, I'll call them both and you can remember them any way you choose!

Mind/Revelational Gifts

- **Word of Wisdom-** This is when verses leap off the page and you have a personal understanding of the meaning for you. The Holy Spirit can make the bible relate to your life in an instant!

When I was a new believer, the first Bible that I owned was a leatherbound NLT Life Application Bible. I wore out that thing so much that from Peter to the end of Revelation was all ripped out and loosely held together by a binder clip and secured in the Bible by a large rubber band. I wrote all over that Bible and I love to read my notes in the margins. I would open to a page that would have "WOW, WOW, WOW, WOW" in the margin next to an underlined verse. Then I would read it again, years later, and wonder what I found so incredible about it. LOL. It certainly spoke to me that day! Today, a completely different verse would likely inspire me!

- **Word of Knowledge-** This is the ability to know something that you shouldn't know about a thing or a person. Jesus demonstrated this gift when He had a conversation with the woman at the well... (See John 4)

The gifts of Word of Knowledge and Prophecy often go hand in hand. As in the example above. When Jesus received information from God the Father about this woman, He was exercising the Gift of the Word of Knowledge. When He shared it with her, He was exercising the Gift of Prophecy.

Not every Word of Knowledge is intended to be shared, however. My friend Nancy shared that she had passed on a Word of Knowledge to her son. He asked her how she knew what she told him. She said she got it from God. Her son had her committed to an institution for this. The people in that hospital also thought she was crazy.

Years later, when she told me the story, I asked her if God told her to share it. She admitted that she didn't even ask Him. When you receive a Word of Knowledge, always thank God for revealing it to you, and then ask Him what you are supposed to do about it. Sometimes you are to pray. Other times you are to share it. Obey His voice.

- **Discerning Spirits-** This gift helps you know whose voice you are listening to. Is the voice, thought, or action from God, the enemy, or you?

Key questions you can ask to test the spirit and grow in this gift are: Is that true in Biblical principle? Is this a false doctrine? Does this line up with God's character, His Names, or His promises? Is it intended to encourage, edify, purify, or uplift? Or does it lead to fear, anxiety, depression, and distress? Discernment grows when you spend time in the Word and in God's presence. God authored the entire Bible. Being tuned in to Holy Spirit will lead you to greater discernment. He knows ALL truth.

Mouth/Vocal Gifts

- **Speaking in Tongues**- This gift is wildly misunderstood, dismissed, and often discouraged. The primary purpose of tongues is to demonstrate surrendering your mouth and praying perfect prayers to God while He is praying perfect prayers over you. It connects you directly with the Heart of God and ensures you are not getting in His way. When used as a tool of prophecy, it is given in public settings. But mostly it is an intimate exchange between you and God. (See 1 Corinthians 14)

There are 40 verses in 1 Corinthians 14 that explain tongues. There are two purposes for the gift of tongues to be used for you or others. If it is for you, it is to uplift and edify you. If for others, it is a means of prophecy when interpreted. Many denominations will throw the baby out with the bathwater by misunderstanding.

When the tongues are given as a prophetic message for others, then an interpreter is needed. This is that context:

> 1 Corinthians 14:18-19 [18] I thank God that I speak in [unknown] tongues more than all of you; [19] nevertheless,

in public worship I would rather say five *understandable* words in order to instruct others, than ten thousand words in a tongue [which others cannot understand].

Mostly, praying in unknown tongues is a private prayer between you and God for edifying and blessing you and God. It is a surrendering of your mouth to the Lord. I think God uses long-dead languages as our spiritual languages so we can't try to learn them and get in His way.

I prayed diligently for the activation of the gift of tongues for about six months. One day, I just started speaking in my heavenly language to my cat! Years later, the Lord reminded me of a nonsense song that I sang to my kids every day at bedtime. He confirmed that I had been singing in tongues for more than 30 years without knowing it!

If you have not yet activated your gift of tongues and would like to, here is a two-part video resource by Dr. Mark Virkler that will walk you through the process of praying for the activation of your heavenly language. This is the link to Dr. Mark Virkler's two-part video series on the tongues. Part 1 https://youtu.be/N3mb8gJyLzU Part 2 https://youtu.be/yD-v03YL7rc [27]

- **Interpretation of Tongues-** This gift is the ability to understand what the Lord is speaking through tongues. It is typically used to interpret prophetic messages given through an unknown language. The interpretation of tongues can be for knowable or unknowable languages.

In Acts 2 a recounting of the events in the upper room where 120 people were waiting for the promised gift of the Holy Spirit, there were an estimated 80 languages. Yet, each heard God's messages in their own language.

---

[27] Dr. Mark Virkler's 2 part video series on the activation of the gift of tongues. Part 1 https://youtu.be/N3mb8gJyLzU Part2 https://youtu.be/yD-v03YL7rc https://CWGMinistries.org

Acts 2:6-8 [6] And when this sound was heard, a crowd gathered, and they were bewildered because each one was hearing those in the upper room speaking in his own language *or* dialect. [7] They were completely astonished, saying, "Look! Are not all of these who are speaking Galileans? [8] Then how is it that each of us **hears in our own language *or* native dialect**? [9]

I remember having an experience like this while in the theater watching *The Passion of the Christ* movie. The entire movie was subtitled. I remembered being aware of having to read the English words quickly. It was kind of stressful! Then later in the movie, I realized that I was hearing it in English and wondered why the subtitles were needed. I specifically remember noticing this in the scene where Pilot and his wife were having a conversation about her dream. I remember discussing it afterward with someone wondering if they noticed the sections that were in English. And I realized there weren't any! It wasn't spoken in English, I simply *heard it* in English.

Linda, a colleague of mine from Christian Leadership University was taking an intercessory prayer class that challenged the students to work up to three hours a day of praying in tongues. One day, she simply asked the Lord what she was saying. She was still speaking in her heavenly language, but her mind was understanding in English. God was speaking faith, hope, and love over her! She wondered why it took her so long to ask for that interpretation!

- **Prophecy-** As stated already, receiving messages from the Lord and sharing them are two different gifts. A prophecy is a message inspired by God, a divine revelation. When you share what God directs you to say, you are exercising the gift of prophecy.

All prophecy is intended to bless, encourage and edify, even if the message is a warning. Much of God's prophetic messages are about the near future. Jonah received a prophetic message about the impending destruction of Ninevah with a call to repentance. Because the people repented and turned from their wicked ways, God spared them. (See Jonah) Other Bible stories tell of different outcomes when people did not heed the warnings and obey them. God's messages are given to help us to know His will so we can obey it.

Often it is as simple as the Lord directing you to generally share a blessing He has given you for others to release His love to them. It's not more complicated than speaking encouragement and edification into their lives.

Who might you have the authority to speak over? You have the authority to speak over your family, anyone under your realm of responsibility, or anyone for whom you have influence. Always and only share what the Lord directs you to share. Sometimes messages are given so you will know how to pray for someone. Often, the Lord will give me messages for my students. That is an example of a seasonal authority. Once a person is not my student, I won't get messages for them anymore.

As mentioned in the last chapter about the Offices, people can grow in different levels of authority, and then they can give messages to broader populations. Lance Wallnau, for example, receives messages for the Christians in the United States and Lana Vawser receives messages on behalf of the Spirit-led body of Christ worldwide.

Hands/Power Gifts

Faith- The ability to believe in God even for salvation is a gift. To exercise the gift of faith is to simply know that if God says it, it's true. Activated faith has the power to pull down heaven to earth.

It is impossible to please God without faith and we are to seek the higher gifts.

> Hebrews 11:6 [6] But without faith it is impossible to [walk with God and] please Him, for whoever comes [near] to God must [necessarily] believe that God exists and that He rewards those who [earnestly and diligently] seek Him.

The Faith Challenge

Gifts are given by the Holy Spirit according to your faith. I had a theory that asking God to increase the gift of faith consistently will lead to an increase in the manifestation of all other Holy Spirit gifts. I issued this challenge for 30 days, and I encourage you to take it now as well.

Every day for 30 days, Ask God out loud as often as the Lord prompts you to increase the gift of faith in your heart that day. Praying with expectancy something like, **"Lord, increase the gift of faith in my heart today. Align my heart with your will so I may bear the fruit I need to for this day. Thank you for what you are doing in me and through me. In Jesus' Name, Amen"**

Thirty-seven people participated in this faith challenge and many experienced amazing miracles. The challenge proved my theory true. People reported an increased boldness to witness to others with salvation stories, some began speaking in tongues, others were given increased prophecies and many saw miracles and healings!

Take the Faith Challenge

The Lord says to expect miracles when we pray by God's will. I am anticipating that this month will change your life! And I'm excited that the Lord has given this sowing and reaping challenge to show us what He can do when we believe Him for his Word.

Putting this prayer on post-it notes in places like the car, your desk, on the bathroom mirror, and the fridge will help prompt multiple opportunities to speak this prayer out loud every day.

One of the things I learned is that because the Holy Spirit comes in fullness, it doesn't matter which of the manifestation gifts you ask for an increase. What you really get is HIM! And when He shows up, there is always MORE supernatural evidence of His blessings! I like the emphasis on faith though, because if you believe God for His promises, you more easily align with His will!

The Gift of Healing

The entire last book in this series, *Encountering the HEALING of God* dives deeply into this gift. God's supernatural healing addresses physical, mental, emotional, and spiritual needs.

One of the reasons I believe so many people have trouble finding their healing is role confusion. God has His part in healing, and you have yours. Misunderstanding the roles and responsibilities can cause frustration and disillusionment.

God's Job

God gives us the direction, the promises, the ability, and the power to receive healing. The Lord gives a clear direction on how to access healing in the Word. There is no puppet string control with God. He sent us the indwelling Holy Spirit as our internal guide to show us the way. Even the faith and power to believe and cooperate with God are from Him. He gives us the conditions for receiving the blessed promises. Then shows us how to do our part to cooperate with His will for our lives.

Your Job

There are only a few things God cannot do. He can't lie or deny Himself or His character. God cannot break a promise. And He can't do your job for you!

The Father didn't need you to do His job. The Son didn't need you to do His job. But to do His job, the Holy Spirit requires your cooperation. If you aren't willing to do your part for yourself, there will be consequences. Your God-given free will enables you to choose to cooperate with Him.

Your job is to listen to God and obey His voice. You exercise your free will by accepting the gift of salvation and faith and welcoming the indwelling Holy Spirit. You need to acknowledge that the power to believe does not come from you. It's a gift from God. You cannot try or muster up the faith in yourself for healing. God has the power to heal supernaturally, and He shares this ability with you by this manifestation gift. To experience it, you must surrender and tap into it.

By spending time with Jesus and the Word of God, you begin to know the Truth. That's how to find the promises for which you are anchoring your life. Being in God's Presence fills up your spiritual tank with His grace and anointing. Ask for the conditions for your healing and obey them. Surrender your own will, so there is room for God's power to be released in and through you.

The Gift of Miracles

If you are a true born-again believer, signs wonders, and miracles should follow you.

> Mark 16:17-18 [17] These signs will accompany those who have believed: in My name they will cast out demons, they will speak in new tongues; [18] they will pick up serpents, and if they drink anything deadly, it will not hurt them; they will lay hands on the sick, and they will get well."

We learn in this next verse that our witnessing should be accompanied by the miraculous power of signs and wonders.

> Romans 15: 18-19 [18] For I will not [even] presume to speak of anything except what Christ has done through me [as an instrument in His hands], resulting in the obedience of the Gentiles [to the gospel], by word and deed, [19] with the power of signs and wonders, [and all of it] in the power of the Spirit.

Many people are unaware that miracles should be part of the everyday Christian experience. I asked the Lord the general question about miracles: What moves You to move in the miraculous through us? He gave me this list of 16 things.

Here was Jesus' list!

- *When you show Me your childlike faith!*
- *When you connect with My heart and seek My will.*
- *When you ask, seek, and knock. Persistently and don't give up.*
- *When you see Me as bigger than your fear or worldly limitations.*
- *When you agree with My promises.*

- *When you Have a heart of gratitude regardless of the waiting period and continually speak in agreement with my promises.*

- *When you testify about Me with boldness and without the fear of man stopping you.*

- *When you take a step of faith toward the promise that proves that you believe Me.*

- *When what you ask for is coming from a pure heart of love, My heart of love! (selfless)*

- *When you ask for what you need from My perspective, and not what you want from your perspective.*

- *When it will increase the faith of the people watching so they can see Me as real.*

- *When you know who you are and step out with the confidence and authority you have in Christ.*

- *When you expect Me to be who you know I am and know who you are in Me.*

- *When you demonstrate spiritual maturity by giving Me the glory and not taking credit for it yourself.*

- *When your eyes are fixed on Me so you can see from My heavenly perspective.*

- *When you understand My timing is strategic and is always perfect.*

That's a powerful list. And can be used as a diagnostic tool. The word "when" reveals that God is showing you the conditions. When you meet HIS conditions, He MUST move because He is a promise keeper and needs to behave consistently with His nature and character. All you must do is ask Him what those conditions are and obey them. Then you can patiently EXPECT Him to show up as a Miracle Worker.

The Positioning Anointing

Timing is everything! If you want to see God show up, you must pay attention to the timing of His assignments and commands. The Lord had given me a concept He called the positioning anointing. This is what He said about it.

> *The positioning anointing is recognizing the assignment I have given you at the time that it is given. It is the window of time where My anointing is present to accomplish the assignment.*
>
> *This can be piece by piece, step by step, as in large assignments like building a Kingdom business, ministry, or writing a book. This is why asking Me to order your day is so important. Working on only what I tell you to do when I tell you ensures that you have the positioning anointing to accomplish it.*
>
> *It can also be one-time opportunities like obeying the prompt to call and forgive someone or talking to a stranger about salvation in a store or on the street. Sensing the timing is important because it is in alignment with Me where the power exists to accomplish it.*
>
> *Delayed obedience is disobedience. Getting ahead of Me or lagging behind Me is acting without My power. It is critically important to listen and obey when you feel the call to do so as then you know I have positioned you to accomplish it. Remember, it's not you alone or Me alone, it's Me working through you to accomplish the Father's will. So take courage and watch what We can do together!*

My sister Michele and I were talking in the parking lot after one of our Spirit Life Circle meetings. She loves to share my books with people and was getting some from the back of my trunk.

A man was sitting in the car next to ours with his window open. After I left, Michele leaned into the car and gave John a book. She invited him to join us next week in the same place, blessed him, and left.

The next week, John sat outside waiting for me to come out of the coffee shop. He approached me and shared that Michele's intervention saved his life. He was sitting in his car, contemplating suicide and crying out to God to show him if He was real. The timely act of offering him the book and the book itself, allowed John to personally encounter God and gave him hope. Had Michele ignored her prompting from the Holy Spirit, perhaps God would have used someone else to connect John to Him. But it was her assignment!

Delayed obedience is disobedience. When you obey God's prompting immediately, you show Him that He can trust you with other assignments. This is how you grow from glory to glory, anointing to anointing.

> 2 Corinthians 3:18 [18] And we all, with unveiled face, *continually* seeing as in a mirror the glory of the Lord, are *progressively* being transformed into His image from [one degree of] glory to [even more] glory, which comes from the Lord, [who is] the Spirit.

One of the reasons we don't obey is that we think it's just us. We focus on our fears and limitations and talk ourselves out of the assignment, justifying the decision. Whenever you have a prompt to do something, no matter how scary, it will **always** be empowered by God. Don't get in God's way by thinking it's all up to you.

190

Encountering the Supernatural Provider

Manifestation Gifts in Me

- Meet Jehovah Jireh in your special place and spend some time enjoying him for a bit.

- Ask Him to show you or tell you which manifestation gifts He tends to release in you the most.

- Ask Him which He wants you to grow in and pray for an increase, or activation of that or those gifts.

- Allow Him to share with you how He will use those gifts in the execution of your calling. Look to see what He shows you and record it in your journal.

- Ask as many clarifying questions as you need to be clear about the direction He is giving you.

Radical Obedience

- Meet Jehovah Jireh in your special place and spend time having fun with Him.

- Ask Jesus; What step have you asked me to take that I have not taken? What action do You want me to take that would require radical obedience on my part?

- Show me how you would equip me to take that step and increase my faith to rise to that challenge.

Open the Eyes of My Heart

- Meet Jehovah Jireh in your special place. Sit or swing with Him for a few minutes, head on His chest, relaxing in His presence.

- Then ask Him to explain Ephesians 1:18 Amplified Bible [18] And [I pray] that the eyes of your heart [the very center and core of your being] may be enlightened [flooded with light by the Holy Spirit] so that you will know *and* cherish the [a]hope [the divine guarantee, the confident expectation] to which He has called you, the riches of His glorious inheritance in the [b]saints (God's people),

- Ask the Lord to apply the truth of this verse by opening the eyes of your heart to see His provisional guidance, resources, or how He has equipped you for a challenge you are facing.

The Sound of a Life Changing by Matthew West

https://youtu.be/XLMEPNDZnhY

DIRECTION
Book Conclusion

⤝⤜

here is a sense of urgency in my heart for you to step into your called destiny. We are privileged to live in an important kingdom season. The Lord is getting ready for His return, and He needs all hands on deck for that preparation.

The intention of this book was as a journey for you to find your true purpose and identity, and what God has uniquely designed you to do for His kingdom plan. It is the heart cry prayer:

Lord, help me to know who you are, be who You need me to be, see what You see, say what needs to be said, and do what needs done. Help me to unite with you and others to accomplish your will. Let my life be a light in this dark world, shining unapologetically for your sake. In Jesus' Name. Amen.

It's time for you to rise as a fully equipped warrior!

The Armor of God

> Ephesians chapter 6:10-20 [10] In conclusion, be strong in the Lord [draw your strength from Him and be empowered

through your union with Him] and in the power of His [boundless] might. [11] Put on the full armor of God [for His precepts are like the splendid armor of a heavily-armed soldier], so that you may be able to [successfully] stand up against all the schemes and the strategies and the deceits of the devil. [12] For our struggle is not against flesh and blood [contending only with physical opponents], but against the rulers, against the powers, against the world forces of this [present] darkness, against the spiritual forces of wickedness in the heavenly (supernatural) places.

[13] Therefore, put on the complete armor of God, so that you will be able to [successfully] resist and stand your ground in the evil day [of danger], and having done everything [that the crisis demands], to stand firm [in your place, fully prepared, immovable, victorious]. [14] So stand firm and hold your ground, having [b]tightened the wide band of truth (personal integrity, moral courage) around your waist and having put on the breastplate of righteousness (an upright heart), [15] and having [c]strapped on your feet the gospel of peace in preparation [to face the enemy with firm-footed stability and the readiness produced by the good news]. [16] Above all, lift up the [protective] [d]shield of faith with which you can extinguish all the flaming arrows of the evil one. [17] And take the helmet of salvation, and the sword of the Spirit, which is the Word of God.

[18] With all prayer and petition pray [with specific requests] at all times [on every occasion and in every season] in the Spirit, and with this in view, stay alert with all perseverance and petition [interceding in prayer] for all [e]God's people. [19] And pray for me, that words may be given to me when I open my mouth, to proclaim boldly the mystery of the good news [of salvation], [20] for which I am an ambassador in chains. And pray that in proclaiming it I may speak boldly and courageously, as I should.

The armor is not just for your protection, which is a defensive posture. But it gives you the confidence to live as a leader offensively. Notice that the Word is the only weapon. You must write the Word on your heart as a holy habit, to have it ready at all times to wield that sword. Will you be ready to live with clear and anointed words and actions? Will you have the Truth stored in your heart so the Holy Spirit can bring the right powerful scriptures when needed?

This is a season where the Lord wants to see the body of Christ rise to become who He created them to be. In a recent Spirit Life Circle, we asked the question; Lord, what would it look like if I lived my life fully alive to your will and destiny for me?

I saw myself as my five-year-old inner child wearing a superhero garment. My hands were on my hips looking straight up with confidence with Jesus holographically covering me. Fearless. Bold. Unapologetic. Supernatural is my natural. I was living a lifestyle marked by abiding, evidenced by signs, wonders, and miracles. I could see so clearly in the spiritual realm that I knew how to both offensively and defensively battle in the spirit. The enemy was afraid of me, because when they looked at me they saw Jesus.

Below is a film clip from the movie *"Robin Hood,"* a character whose exploits have endured in popular mythology and ignited the imagination of those who share his spirit of adventure and righteousness. In 13th century England, Robin and his band of marauders confront corruption in a local village and lead an uprising against the crown that will forever alter the balance of world power. And whether thief or hero, one man from humble beginnings became an eternal symbol of freedom for his people.

This clip from the movie addresses the seed planted by his father in a young Robin's heart that lambs need to become lions.

Robin Hood: Lambs become Lions
https://bit.ly/3PVhuux

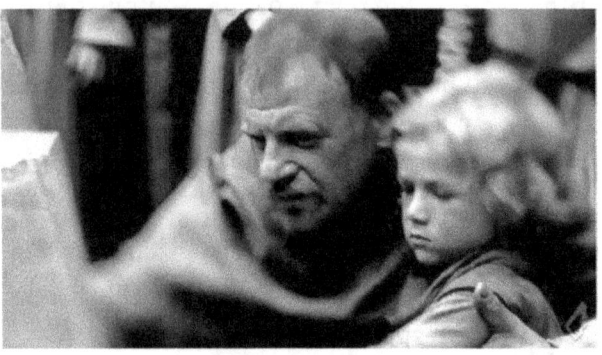

Frozen Skipping Stones- Your Present State

The Lord took me back to the Sea of Galilee where he first showed me the skipping stones. Once again, He handed me a smooth stone and I skipped it. It bounced and as it began to multiply. it froze in midair. He asked me to throw a few more; they all did the same thing. They were all frozen in a multiple skipped mode.

> *You have begun the work that I've called you to do. These stones represent the people I've put in your path, seeds planted in the hearts of people for whom you share my light. These stones are beginning to skip multiply. This is a picture of your present stage.*

> *You are growing in increased boldness and confidence to simply share your stories. As you allow Me to clean out your heart, you reach the new levels of anointing. You are doing well to abide in Me. Soon you will receive much more of My presence and power in your life as you continue to grow in your relationship with Me. Don't compare yourself with others. This is your journey, and we are mapping it out together.*

Thank you so much for being my Lord, my Author, and my Shepherd. I love the way you are writing my life!

Kingdom Plan Big Picture–

Here is an adventure and conversation that the Lord gave me that clarifies His Kingdom plan.

My five-year-old self woke up in my special place one morning to my angel Maureen telling me that the Lord had a special adventure planned for me. As Maureen and I packed my little blue 1960s suitcase, I put the lion stuffed animal in there. It shouldn't have fit, but it somehow did. I thought that was funny. Other angels made the bed, I loved that!

Maureen took me to a place where Jesus was standing next to a helicopter. He picked me up with a big smile and lifted me into the helicopter without telling me where we were going. It didn't matter. I knew it would be amazing!

We flew up over the waterfall in the river of living water where all the destiny caves peppered the walls. I was trying to work out which one was mine. There were simply too many to be able to guess. The walls of the river gorge seemed to be miles high, and I could not see the top.

There were vivid iridescent strings like a beautiful giant spirograph connecting to the cave openings. We were flying right through them without disrupting them with our movement. The strings were of different thicknesses, some thick like cables and others thin like spiderwebs. I asked Jesus to tell me what the strings were.

This is a picture of my kingdom plan being executed in unity by the body of Christ!

It's beautiful and complex, Lord.

Each string represents relationships and partnerships between members of the body of Christ. The thinner ones can be as simple as a chance encounter, the seed planted in the heart. The thicker ones represent hand-in-hand ministry cooperation. There are thousands, millions, and in some cases billion of connections that a single person may have with others. Many of these connections they will not even realize until the end of days. But all of them are known and remembered by Me.

Unity is very important in this season. My power is magnified and multiplied by unity, first with Me and then with others in the body of Christ. The season for individual ministries is finished. We are in the season of the great awakening. No one can accomplish what I have called them to do alone.

We are approaching the great harvest of nations which must come before the tribulation and My return. For those who serve with selfless motives, I will give the double portion of Billy Graham's anointing and multiply it further by their partnership. My math is exponential.

The next thing I knew, we were in the throne room. Jesus was sitting on the throne high and massive with fire eyes and I was with Maureen seeing the 24 elders and the Angels roaring HOLY, HOLY, HOLY! It was a powerful and humbling site!

Then King Jesus stood up! His standing was a call to action! The words UNITY, HUMILITY, SELFLESSNESS, OBEDIENCE, JOY, FAITHFULNESS, and LOVE roared in my spirit and kept repeating themselves.

When the vision was over, I was back in my special place with Jesus. Whoa, Lord, that was very cool and intense! Thank you for that adventure. Why did I need to pack my suitcase?

Because I want your heart to always be ready to go when I call. To obey every assignment and to trust Me for each one.

Yes, Lord. I will!

Lord, I love to see those massive connections between the body of Christ. Help me to connect to everyone I need to fulfill my part of your plan.

Stay tuned to Me so that you are aware when I'm making a connection. I set the table in the presence of your enemies! I go before you and prepare the hearts of the people that need to connect with you in advance.

Thank you, Lord, and increase my awareness of your plans and connections! In Jesus' Name, Amen!

Have Courage -Holographic Cards Vision

One day in my local Spirit Life Circle after a discussion about courage, we used this verse as a prompt to ask the Lord more about it in journaling.

Deuteronomy 31:6 Be strong and courageous, do not be afraid or tremble in dread before them, for it is the LORD your God who goes with you. He will not fail you or abandon you."

Our Journal Question that day was: Lord, what do you want to show me or say to me about having the courage to represent you as Your "face" in my circle of influence?

The Lord showed me holographic cards. The kind that changes the picture from one thing to another when you move the card slightly. The images had movement, like those live photos on your phone that can show you a few seconds of movement and then stop.

The cards shifted from me to Jesus and there was that one way to hold the card where I could see both of us superimposed on each other. There were four cards.

- The first was an image of Jesus and me wearing armor. There was a wind blowing our hair beneath the helmet.

- Next, we were wearing Doctor scrubs. We were performing heart surgery.

- In the third, we dressed as gardeners, bent down in a garden and there were garden tools near us. We had an especially broad smile on our faces in this one.

- The fourth was us geared up for fishing with the thigh-high boots, rods, and a tackle box.

I need you to be the face to those for whom I have put in your path to reflect Me in your culture as the Warrior, the Healer, the Sower and Reaper, and the Fisher of Men.

When they see you, I want them to see Me. The Warrior teaches them to find their strength by connecting to the Almighty source of all strength. There is no fear or worry when they can connect with this aspect of Me. This is the pathway to victory. I AM the Shield, the Banner, and the one who Fights their battles. Show them the way.

When they see you, I want them to see Me. You have met the Healer and know how to introduce others to Him. You know My heart for healing and can show people how to trust Me as their Healer too. It is important to release My healing power to a hurting and wounded generation. Show them the way.

When they see you, I want them to see Me. You have a heart for discipleship, a yearning for people to live the fullness of

God in their lives and not leave Me dormant in their hearts. Just as a Gardener, you show people how to plant the seeds of My love in their hearts, nurture and grow their relationship with Me and then release Me into the world. This is the fruit-bearing of the Kingdom plan, multiplying and growing My love. Show them the way.

When they see you, I want them to see Me. We are approaching the Great Harvest. So many people need Me. Even the people who think they have Me need Me. Your life must be a contagious reflection of My Love, a magnetic attraction so that the Fisherman's boat is overcome with fish. People need to know how to live the Gospel in their lives and lead others to this hungering heart's desire. Show them the way.

Thank you, Lord, for this powerful imagery and encounter. Thank you for fully equipping me to be able to do as you ask. I say "yes" and "amen" to all that you would have me do to reflect your love in these ways. In Jesus' Name, Amen.

To reflect God's love in this world takes courage. But know that courage is not mustered in your own strength. The Lord Himself is the source of the courage and the power to be His face in your circle of influence.

What God Showed Others

Protecting your Purpose (Kathryn Lapp)

I AM THAT I AM. I am whatever you need Me to be in your circumstances to fulfill your destiny in the Kingdom of God. Your little part in My great Kingdom is important to Me. Do not minimize it. Like a knitted garment needs every stitch to make its pattern, not one of them can be dropped or else the pattern is broken; so I need you to hold your place and stand your ground in My Kingdom.

My grace is so great that, even if you stumble, I can work that into the pattern too. Romans 8:28 - All things work together for good. So, I will be whatever you need Me to be to protect your purpose in My Kingdom. I will protect you, I will provide for you, take care of you, guide you, and walk with you. When you feel weak, you are strong with Me.

The Commissioning (Anonymous)

Jesus lifted me up into the clouds. We are walking, and He is holding my hand as we walk. I can see the clouds in front of me but as soon as we arrive, Jesus parts them like a curtain.

We go through the first one and I see fire burning and it is so hot in there that I'm hoping we're not there very long. Jesus is holding my hand and we walked right through the fire, not around it, but through it. If He wasn't holding my hand I would have run back. I'm silent and I'm walking but I'm not getting burned. Jesus stops and He picks me up and hugs me as we are standing in the middle of a blazing fire.

After what seemed like a long while there, He finally walked toward the cloud again, and its parts, and then we are on another cloud. I am not burned. Jesus' robe is still white, and I'm surprised by that.

We are then walking to a waterfall. I saw this place before. It's inviting with the breeze, and it sure feels a lot better than the fire. Jesus is still holding me as we head for the waterfall.

There are rocks and we are descending down a steep path to get to the water. We reached the water and it's beautiful. Without Jesus, I wouldn't have made it down the steep hill. He finally speaks.

Always trust Me (nickname). I AM pleased with you when you cling to Me and allow Me to lead you through the trials in your life. You may be afraid, but if you hold onto Me, and abide in Me I will lead you in My ways. Don't doubt it.

He puts me down and says;

I wanted you to see the fire you have been walking through and know that I hold you. See the fire you have been walking through? Know I hold your hand whenever I'm burning the dross from your soul. Then I lead you to the living waters to refresh you. Drink deeply and be refreshed.

We are sitting on a rock and Jesus gets up and goes to the water. He didn't take my hand or tell me to follow but left me sitting on the rock. He was enjoying the water. It seems so refreshing after the fire. I carefully went closer to the water's edge and hesitantly went in after Him. And then He said,

I was wondering if you'd follow Me. You are ready.

Ready for what? I asked.

The next upstep. Trust Me. When the time comes, you'll see.

We were both enjoying the water and I follow Jesus through the waterfall to the back. Water was now falling in front of us, and my hair was soaked, and we were sitting on a Ridge watching the falls. Jesus walked to the ledge, and I followed, and we were out of the water walking on the opposite side of the lake on a flat grassy meadow toward another cloud. As soon as I reached it, the cloud parted, and we were in a beautiful temple of gold. Angels were surrounding us as I looked up. There were others there excited to see Jesus. He introduced me by my name as My faithful servant.

They welcomed me.

I wanted you to meet her.

I'm filled with joy and feel instantly accepted.

> *It's time for her anointing. She has been faithful so now she is ready for the next upstep.*

Jesus sits on his throne and He has me sit next to Him. Someone brings Him a gold small container and he dips his right finger in it and puts anointing oil on my forehead.

> *This anointing oil I put on your head as a symbol of My power and My authority for you to be used for My glory. Remember you are My vessel for My use. Because you are faithful, I AM now going to increase My power in you. These are my witnesses. Remember to only do and say the things you see Me doing. Stay close to Me. Be holy as I AM holy and accept this calling from Me. I've called you to do My perfect will. Do you accept this calling in the presence of My servants who will help you?*

I do Jesus, I want more of You and to serve You as You desire for Your glory. Thank you for the privilege and your love. Thank you for not giving up on me. Even though I am weak, you work with my weakness. This is how I know it is from You. Keep me from pride and temptation so I may never think that it's me alone. I am yours. Use me.

Cheerios and the Supernatural Provider- (Pamela White)

Many years ago, when I was very new in the Lord and just learning who God was, He walked me through a situation that allowed me to experience Him as Jehovah Jireh, my Supernatural Provider.

My family lived in the beautiful flat prairie land of the Midwest where the wind blows freely, and you can see for miles standing on your front porch. At the time, I was a stay-at-home mom raising our four children. I'm not sure of the motive, but my husband decided he would no longer provide money for groceries. Suddenly I could not depend on my husband for food. I had to turn to God for provision.

Since we lived in the country, I was able to plant a large garden that brought us fruits and vegetables, so we were not starving. The Lord abundantly blessed our garden. It was a time of drought. While our neighbors were struggling to get a few green beans, a few ears of corn, and a radish or two, our garden was overflowing. I placed canned fruits and vegetables until it was packed full, and my shelves were fully stocked. I had so much, that I gave to the neighbors whose gardens were not producing.

Sometimes, it would have been nice to have something besides a very strict vegetable diet to give the children. We were fine though. The Lord kept us healthy and safe. We did not feel hunger pangs. I thanked the Lord every day for providing food for my children.

Occasionally, the Lord would speak to friends and neighbors and suddenly we would find a box or bags of groceries sitting on our porch. They would have fun stuff we were not used to eating, like macaroni or cereal. Once a bag of groceries had a box of Cheerios. My children thoroughly enjoyed those Cheerios. It had been a long time since they had eaten cereal.

With four children and myself eating Cheerios, you would think the box would empty quickly. It certainly felt empty. When the next mealtime came around, the children wanted a Cheerios treat again. I remember reaching for the box and thanking the Lord for the joy the Cheerios had brought the children and was thankful for something to eat besides green beans.

Every time I poured from that box I cried in gratefulness. Our box of Cheerios lasted for many months. It felt empty every time I picked up the box and every time I poured it; it filled every child's bowl.

Our Cheerios reminded me of the account of the widow in 1 Kings 17, who only had a little flour and a little oil. She was going to make a cake, then she and her son were going to starve to death. God sent the prophet Elijah to her home, and he instructed her to make him a cake first. She obeyed and her flour and oil did not run dry until the Lord again rained on the land.

Our box of Cheerios did not run dry during our time of need. My God showed himself as Jehovah Jireh, my Provider, in blessing my garden, sending groceries to our door, and even giving my children a desire of their heart as well as nutrients they needed through an always sustaining box of Cheerios.

Increase my Holy Boldness/Walk on Water- Cindy Fiebig

Lord, how can I increase my holy boldness in my circle of influence?

Lord, You know that I am thinking that this is the whole point of the business/ministry You are leading me to launch. You Are leading me to use crochet as a "hook" to reel women in, so that I can share the gospel of Your love with them. But I'm not there yet. What is the answer to this question for where I am right now? I want so much to be aware of Your Presence with me always.

> *When you are aware of Me with you, you can share that with whoever you are with, even (names) or your neighbors or store clerks or anyone! As you become more comfortable with sensing My abiding Presence, you will become bolder about speaking about Me to others.*

Right now, you hesitate to mention Me or what I AM doing because your eyes are on yourself. Stop and breathe. See Me with you, in you. Stop and listen and look to see what I AM communicating to you, then do what you see, hear, and feel Me releasing to you. Wherever you are, whoever you are with, release My love to them. I love all of you and I want to use you to communicate My love to them.

Don't hesitate to follow Me. Yes, I AM calling you to walk on the water with Me. I put you in Patty's group because she understands the value of stepping out on the deep. Don't be afraid.

If now you could see the future, I have planned for you, you would know that fear cannot be a part of it. Learn NOW how to keep the eyes of your heart fixed on Me as I ask you to step out and do what man thinks is not possible. All things are possible to him who believes – and that is you.

Come walk on the water with Me.

I hear You telling me that You have called me to a special place in Your Body. All of us in this generation are special, are Your warriors, but You have something even more for me than what I am expecting from all of us. Jesus, take me! Take me! Please show me who I am in You.

(I Hear the Oceans song by Hillsong United)

I see the waves crashing down. I see You standing out in the distance, and You Are walking toward me.

Now You Are here, reaching out Your Hand to me. You Are lifting me out of the boat, and I am standing up. I step out, first with my right foot, then I look full into Your Face. I feel my left foot step on the water.

Come with Me to the great unknown. I know all things and I call you to come with Me.

You are holding both of my hands and we are walking one step at a time. You Are drawing me back toward You. I can hear the waves, but I am looking at You.

I am standing with You in the distance, and You wave Your Hand out over the horizon. I see lands, islands, and maybe shores of distant lands, and I know that You Are saying this is the ground You have for me to plant a seed in.

Then You lift me above Your head like I am a child, and You are playing with me. I can see the lands more clearly because I can see farther inland. I know I am safe because You are holding me, and I am resting on You.

I look into Your Eyes. Then I put my head against Your chest, and I cling to You.

I find myself back in the boat. I fall down and worship You, God Almighty.

Putting it all together: Finding God's Direction in your Life

Hopefully, you have had many enlightening encounters with Jesus as you worked through the five Names of God in this book. Here are some key questions you can ask yourself to help you Find God's Direction in your life. Answer these questions using only a few words, not in long sentences. It will help you process it all in the end much easier.

How has your past prepared you for God's future in and through you?

- What have you learned from your life stories?

- How has your past affected who you are?

- What lessons have you learned that you can use to help others?

What is the core identity truth that guides you?

- What core value scripture can you use to anchor and guide your life?

- How has God used this scripture to give you clarity about your identity in Him and your purpose?

Who does God want you to serve?

- What is one Motivational Gift God has used to help you see the needs that He wants to use you to meet?

- What people or groups do you have the compassion to serve?

- What issues has God put on your heart that you can relate to this population?

What does God want you to do?

- What skills or natural abilities has God given you that you love to do?

- What Ministry gifts match your abilities?

- What doors has God been opening or people He is connecting you with for service purposes?

- What is God motivating you to specifically do for this population?

What is God's desired Kingdom impact through you?

- What vision(s) has God given me about the impact He has for me?

- Which Manifestation Gifts has God released in you that connect with your natural gifts?

- How would people benefit if you stepped into that calling? (Describe the impact as the Lord shows it to you)

- What step is God giving you today to cooperate with His will for this calling?

Putting all of this together, meditate on all of the answers to these questions and ask the Lord to show you a glimpse of yourself living out this destiny in full cooperation with Him. Then day by day ask Him, what steps or actions do I need to take toward this future today? And follow Him one day at a time.

You have a great responsibility to be a believer living at this time in a fallen world. Carrying the truth and being the light in a dark world is a challenge. You are called to be in this world and not of this world. Your life is intended to be a light in the darkness. When you know your true identity and destiny, you can't help but be light.

Imbibe the Word of God. Allow the truth of who God is and who you are in Him to soak into your bones and cause you to rise up. We are in a generation where the darkness does not comprehend us. Many will resist. This is why it requires courage in Christ to step into the truth of who God has called you to be.

> Matthew 7:24 24 "So everyone who hears these words of Mine and acts on them, will be like a wise man [a far-sighted, practical, and sensible man] who built his house on the rock.

Wise people act according to God's will. Those who dare to act, build their foundation on solid rock. Speak the word in love. Allow Jesus to love through you the way He designed and created you to do so.

> 1 Corinthians 7:23 You were bought with a price [a precious price paid by Christ]; do not become slaves to men [but to Christ].

You were bought at the price of Jesus' shed blood for you. Don't allow your fear of man to limit your kingdom impact. In the end, you will be rewarded by the fruit of your eternal life. How well will you live the life God has for you as part of His ultimate kingdom plan?

That is what God desires for you and me. And the time is ripe for the harvest. So, what are you waiting for?

Appendix A
Dialogue Journaling Tips

Know which voice you are hearing

- **God's Voice– spontaneous positive** thoughts, pictures, and feelings consistent with any Name of God, Character of God, or Nature of God. (Any of the Fruit of the Spirit, "Omni" Truths, and compound Names of God). God can speak through images, stories, emotions, music, and sparks of creative insight... God speaks the language of the heart.

- **Satan's voice– spontaneous negative** thoughts, pictures, and feelings consistent with his character and nature. (Lying, deceiving, tears down, lead you away from faith in God). Listening to this voice will lead to faith in reverse and will amplify worry.

- **Your own thoughts – analytical, practical, logical**. Your thoughts speak in the language of the head. They may even look like a list of practical concerns, but remember, the LORD offers solutions.

Don't expect it to look or sound a certain way. God's ways are different from your ways. Your specific expectations can be a significant barrier to hearing from God. He does not need to sound like a booming voice.

Give God credit for when He speaks to you or shows you something spontaneously. That brilliant idea that came to you in the meeting, for example, was God. Make sure you thank Him for it. Likewise, **don't take credit for negative thoughts** or pictures that are self-deprecating or send you backward in your faith. Those thoughts are from the enemy and the sooner you recognize them and rebuke the enemy out loud, the faster they will cease. Rebuking out loud is important because the enemy is not Omniscient. He doesn't know your thoughts. So, speak with the authority of God when you recognize these negative messages.

Have **spiritual counselors** to help you make sure you are hearing from God. The characteristics of a good spiritual counselor are:

- They should **know the Word, have a close relationship with God, and be able to discern His Voice themselves. They should also be humble enough to have spiritual advisors themselves.**

- **Submit your journaling** to a counselor when **you are learning** how to discern God's voice.

- **Submit your journaling** to a counselor to **people with more experience** in an area where you have specific issues which the LORD is addressing.

- **Submit your journaling** to a counselor when you get a message **that does not seem consistent with God's**

Character. Remember, God's Voice will be full of faith, hope, and love. He will gently and lovingly convict of sin but will not condemn or tear you down.

- **Submit your journaling** to a counselor if it is related to a **major life transition, or if you feel that what you received doesn't feel or sound like God.**

Don't try – Striving to hear from God is you trying in your own effort. This does not work, and you will likely get a journal that analyzes your circumstances logically. This is not from God. You need to relax **and let God take the wheel.** It's much easier than you might expect.

Imagine yourself as a small child. This connects you with your inner child and **awakens childlike faith.**

It doesn't have to be perfect. Don't put off talking to God because you want everything to be perfect and you want to have a lot of time to do it. **It doesn't require a lot of time** to speak to Jesus. A few minutes of quality time with Jesus is much better than not spending time with Him at all.

Avoid evaluating what you are receiving from the LORD as you are getting it. **Evaluation at the moment is doubt.** When you begin to doubt the validity of the experience, you hang up on Jesus. Allow yourself to receive the flow of the Holy Spirit freely, knowing you can evaluate it later.

Evaluate what you have received after your time with Jesus is complete. The message should be consistent with Scripture and the Names and Character of God. God is all about faith, hope, and love. Even if the Lord is giving you constructive discipline, your message from the LORD should build you up, help you feel loved, and give you hope. If it doesn't, then it's worth passing by a spiritual counselor.

How to avoid distractions

Internal distractions like having a lot of things on your mind can be dealt with by pulling out paper and **writing a list of the things that you need to do** so you won't forget them. That way you can literally set them aside and focus on the LORD.

External distractions – Find a place where you know that no one will bother you. If necessary, use noise-canceling earphones or relaxation music with no crescendos. And, no one bothers you in the bathtub. ;-)

Ways to quiet yourself down

Deep breathing- Breathe in the Power of the Holy Spirit, exhale anxiety and other negative thoughts. It's relaxing and helps you focus on Jesus.

Find a **comfortable place and position-** Don't get so comfortable that you fall asleep. Although, God certainly can and does speak to us in dreams! Comfortable means that you are not distracted by pain but are not so relaxed that you fall asleep.

If **music** is helpful, that's great. Just make sure that it is **instrumental and has a steady rhythm**. You don't want the music to lead the experience. That's Jesus' job. The songs in this book are more for worship and meditation which posture your heart for connecting with God. For quiet meditation, however, go with relaxing instrumental songs. I find that "Classic Music for Studying" and "Instrumental Christian" are great Pandora[28] stations for journaling.

Singing or praying in tongues is a wonderful way to get your eyes on Jesus. When you have surrendered your mouth, you can know that the Holy Spirit is fully engaged, and your heart is made ready for Jesus. It is a guaranteed way to make sure that Jesus is taking the wheel. However, if this is not a gift that God has released in you yet, do *not* stress about it or feel that God is not speaking to you. Ask God to open the door for the gift of tongues to be released in you. He will answer that prayer.

Capturing the flow of the Holy Spirit

Always begin by **fixing your eyes on Jesus**. It's OK if you don't see Jesus' face or whole body at first. That is common. But don't let that make you think it's not real or isn't working. Sometimes people can just feel His loving Presence and that's enough. The point is that **He needs to be your focus.**

Speak with an experience only the One True God. Don't pray to your deceased relatives or any other entities. You are speaking to the Father through Jesus, by the power of the Holy Spirit. You can call directly to any Names of the Godhead (Jesus, Heavenly Father, Holy Spirit, or any of God's Names), just don't pray to or worship anyone else.

I encourage you to set the stage for your conversation with Jesus by meeting with Him in **your special place**, for example. But once He is in the scene, **take your hands off the wheel and let Him take over**. The purpose of the special place is to give you an anchoring place to collect memories of Jesus that make it easier to trust that

---

[28] www.Pandora.com

you can see Him again there whenever you need to. You don't need to always see Him there, however. And, God can change your special place over time.

Some people can and like to **write down the conversation** as it is happening. I do this. It's just capturing what the LORD is saying as He is saying it. This is especially important if you are using the ears of your heart to hear Him speak. **Others need to see the scene without pulling out the paper and writing.** When I ask God for a visual experience, I do this. If this is you, then make sure to ask the LORD to help you remember everything important so you can write it down afterward. I want to keep looking and the LORD is faithful to help me remember every detail that I experienced. When the vision is complete, I journal what I saw.

Writing your journal conversations and experiences is important, even if you don't like writing. Your journal provides a **written record** of what the LORD has said and shown you. It is also a log **of your answered prayers**. I always re-read my journals when they are full and it's amazing to remember the experiences I had with Jesus that I may have forgotten.

Remember that this is **a conversation with God**, keep looking, keep talking, and **ask follow-up questions** like you would if you were talking to a friend. Write down the flow of that conversation.

A **song** rolling around in your head can be a message from God. I like to look up the lyrics of a song that is stuck in my head. There is nearly always a message in the lyrics that is exactly what I needed that day.

What to do when you are stuck

Watch how you talk about being stuck. Don't activate faith in reverse by saying out loud that "I can't do this." You can do it; you just need to believe that you can do it because the LORD promises that everyone can do it. **Speak in agreement with what God says.**

Confess and repent of any unbelief and ask God to increase your faith so that you can relax and be able to hear and see Him.

Ask the LORD if there is any unconfessed sin that may be blocking your ability to hear. **Confess and repent of that sin** and try it again.

If you are still stuck, fast and **pray for the LORD to show you** the specific block. You may have a feeling, a person's name pop into your mind, or a conflict that needs to be addressed. Listen and do what He says to get the flow back.

Things to avoid

God is not a genie or a magic 8 ball. For this reason, **avoid asking predictive questions** about your future. The LORD will reveal promises and glimpses of your future when and if He desires. Trust Him one day at a time. Ask Him about today. Matthew 6:11 says; "Give us this day."

Along the same lines, **avoid telling Jesus how you want things to go,** or what you think should happen. This is a learning curve for sure, but things will go much better for you when you learn to let God take control. Keep your attitude humble and faithful.

Great Questions to Ask Jesus

It is helpful to focus your prayer by **calling on the Name of God** that is related to your issue: Some examples are:

- Jehovah Jireh, how can I cooperate with your provision?

- Good Shepherd, what do you want me to do today?

- Comforter, you know every heart and every motivation, show me their heart. Or, Show me my heart.

- Great I AM, You are the Source of all wisdom, please give me wisdom in this circumstance.

- Mighty Counselor, You know the very best course of action for this circumstance; what do you want me to say or do in this situation today?

- LORD, you are the Author of my story, what is the step I can take today to move forward toward the promise you have given me?

- Great Physician, what do I need to do to receive your healing? What is the condition that I need to meet to receive healing?

- Word of God, help me understand these Scripture verses. No one can explain them better than He can.

- Ask Jesus about Biblical concepts like, Abiding in Him, Forgiveness, Surrender, Old Testament concepts and their New Testament parallels, The Trinity, Creation, etc. Anything you want to understand more about your faith, the Bible, and your relationship with Him is OK to ask. He is not too busy to answer these questions. In fact, He delights in answering them.

Pour your heart out to God. You can be brutally honest with God. He knows everything anyway. There's no point in trying to be phony with God. Your best friend wouldn't put up with that, so why should Jesus? After you vent, make sure you pause and listen. This is what made King David the man after God's own heart.

Remember to **let Jesus do most of the talking**. If your journals are filled with your venting and no responses from Jesus, you are missing a huge blessing. This is "dialogue journaling", not "monologue journaling." Dialogue journaling is your prayers with God's response in conversations and experiences. What He has to say is the more important part of the conversation. Also, when the Lord pours His heart out to you, thank Him. **Reply to Him that you understand what He is saying and purpose in your spirit to obey Him.**

Adventures to have with Jesus

- **Enter a Bible scene**- If you have read about an experience that someone had in the Bible, you can ask Jesus to give you this experience. A few nice ones that I have had the pleasure of experiencing were talking with Jesus at the well, walking on water, listening to Jesus give the Sermon on the Mount, and watching David write a psalm. The Bible is full of wonderful stories and Jesus loves to take us on adventures.

- **A shared Bible story experience**- The above idea can also be experienced as a group. My Bible study group experienced the Day of Pentecost by meditating together on Acts 1:1-21. The LORD showed each of us something different and we shared what we saw as we were prompted by Him to do so. Our experiences rounded out a beautiful picture together!

- **Jesus will often take you on adventures** without you asking for them. If He wants you to understand something, He will take you to a place and allow you to experience an activity that will send the exact message that He has for you. **Be willing to follow Him on that adventure.**

- A great healing opportunity is to **ask Jesus to take you to a difficult time in your past** and ask Him to show you either where He was at the time, or give you His perspective on it. Just seeing Him there can be all it takes to lead you to forgiveness.

- **Ask the LORD to give you a picture, story, metaphor, or parable** that will help you understand a Biblical concept or a complicated situation you are facing. This is exactly how Jesus taught people while He was on earth. So, we know that He loves to do that and will do that for you as you work through the encounter exercises in this book. He speaks in your language and brings in elements from your own life to help you understand things.

How to call on the Names and Promises of God

The easiest way to find anything in the Bible is to simply put the search term in any computer browser. If you want scripture about healing, simply put 'verses about healing' for example. I guarantee many people have already written blogs or created lists on this topic for you! If you want to find a Bible story, simply type a search word about it such as 'verses walking on water 'and the verses about Peter's experience will pop up.

For a more in-depth Biblical study, BibleGateway.com has advanced search capacity. In addition to just putting in a keyword, verse, or topic in the main search bar, there is a "keyword search" just below that bar that allows you to search 3 ways: **match all words, match any word, match the exact phrase.** I will indicate below which of those matching keywords I used to come up with the recommended lists accordingly. Play around with this capability. The more specific you are in your keyword search, the more results that match what you are actually looking for will come up.

You may also play around with parallel scriptures or do these search terms with different Bible versions. The app and website have wonderful flexibility.

Finding the Name of God in Scripture:

Perhaps the best overall search for the Names of God is to **search "God is"** (exact phrase). This will give you 1376 verses in the NIV and is a wonderful way to learn in much more detail about the "Is-ness" of God.

- Example: 1 John 4:16 "And so we know and rely on the love God has for us. **God is love.** Whoever lives in love lives in God, and God in them."

Along those lines, the search **"I am"** will return 967 verses in the NIV (exact word order search).

- Example: Genesis 17:1 "When Abram was ninety-nine years old, the LORD appeared to him and said, "**I am God Almighty**; walk before me faithfully and be blameless."

Look for the intention of the Scripture. The verse doesn't need to include the Name of God in it to address the topics or areas of concern under the Name's jurisdiction. **Ask, "What is the key action of this Scripture?"**

- Example: Jeremiah 30:17 "For I will restore you to health And I will heal you of your wounds,' declares the LORD..." The key action of this verse is to restore health and heal a wound. The Great Physician is the Name of God for this verse.

225

To look for the Name of God, I **look at the key action or character** represented in the verse. Is the verse trying to give me comfort? Then the Name of God may be the Comforter. Is the verse giving me wisdom or advice? Then it's probably the Mighty Counselor that is speaking. Is God fighting for me in this verse? Then it may be addressing the Shield, the Banner, or the Mighty Warrior. Is the verse suggesting leading us in a certain direction or giving us guidance in our lives? Perhaps it is referencing the Good Shepherd or the Author. If it's about physical, emotional, mental, or physical needs, then it could be addressing the Great Physician and Healer.

Finding the Promises of God:

To look for a promise in the Bible **look for absolute words** such as 'will', 'always', 'forever' or 'never', as opposed to 'sometimes', 'might' kinds of statements. There are a lot of absolute words in the Bible if you look for them.

- Example: Deuteronomy 31:6 Be strong and courageous. Do not be afraid or terrified because of them, for the LORD your God goes with you; he **will never leave you nor forsake you.**" The promise here is that the LORD will never leave or forsake you!

Searching (all words search) **'promises, God'**. 80 verses will pop up for you in the NIV. Or (all words search) **'covenant, God'** and 81 verses will pop up for that one.

- Example: Psalm 85:8 "I will listen to what **God** the LORD says; He **promises** peace to His people, His faithful servants— but let them not turn to folly."

Finding the Conditions of the Promise:

When looking for conditions of a promise, search for words like **"if,"** **"when," and "then"** kinds of words.

- Example: 2 Chronicles 7:14 "**if** my people, who are called by my Name, will humble themselves and pray and seek my face and turn from their wicked ways, **then** I will hear from heaven, and I will forgive their sin and will heal their land." Humility, seeking God's face, and turning from wicked ways are the conditions required for the promise of healing their land.

"Therefore" is a word that tells me that I need to look for the **context of a promise** or a command. Whenever you see the word, "therefore," ask God, what is that "there for"? Look at a verse or two before to find the context when the word "therefore" is present.

- Example: Matthew 19:67 "So they are no longer two, but one flesh. What **therefore** God has joined together, let no man separate." The unity of the two becoming one flesh is the context for the command for no man to separate them.

Noticing when the conditions are commands.

A **command is a directive language**. You can tell a directive when it begins the sentence and directives are usually commanding verbs. It is intentional and strong.

- Example: Matthew 7:7 "**Ask**, and it **will** be given to you; **seek**, and you **will** find; **knock**, and it **will** be opened to you...." Ask, seek, and knock are the directives. The three uses of "will" show you the promises.

227

Notice that the directives are also the conditions of the promise. You need to cooperate with the Holy Spirit in this verse to receive these promises.

How to pray with authority/without idols in your heart

- Before you pray, do some **Bible research** based on your issue and need. Using the tips above, find the Name, characteristic or topic to research and find His promises categorically.

- **Call on the Name of God** relevant to your circumstance or issue.

- **Praise Him** for what that Name means for this situation.

- **Remind Him Who He is** and what He has promised.

- **Confess and repent** of any anxiety or unbelief that He can take care of in this situation.

- **Speak out loud that you agree with God**'s best plan and His sovereignty in this situation.

- **Ask Him to show you what the conditions** are for the healing or issue to be resolved.

- **Obey His instructions.**

- **Thank Him** for what you will learn and for how He will resolve this situation.

- **Praise Him** and end with "In Jesus' Name, Amen." This is important because you are claiming the authority of Jesus when you pray.

Practice this by taking any of the Names of God in this list and using the Scripture and promised identified, or what you have learned from researching the other search recommendations, write out a prayer that addresses your issue.

Example situation: You have just lost your job unexpectedly and have anxiety about the bills. You want peace in your heart. An example prayer is below the Name listing:

Prince of Peace

Found in: Philippians 4:6-7 ⁶"Do not be anxious about anything, but in every situation, by prayer and petition, with thanksgiving, present your requests to God. ⁷And the peace of God, which transcends all understanding, will guard your hearts and your minds in Christ Jesus."

Promises made by this Name: Peace is part of the Fruit of the Spirit. We can't have it without God. The LORD wouldn't command us not to be anxious if it was impossible. He gives us the instructions in these verses. Surrender all to Him and He will give you peace!

Other Verses or Search Terms

- Isaiah 9:6
- Ephesians 2:11-18
- John 14:27
- John 16:33
- Galatians 5:22
- Peace, God- 42 verses
- Peace, Spirit- 9 verses
- Peace, Jesus- 27 verses

Your Turn Practice Exercises:

Example Prayer: LORD, you are my Prince of Peace. You know that I have lost my job, and You have commanded me not to be anxious. You promise me that You will give me peace in all situations. I thank You for this turn of events because I trust that you are guarding my heart against fear and will bless me with Your Peace in this circumstance. I surrender this situation to You and trust You to guide me in Your Peace. What do You want me to know or to do today to receive Your Peace in this situation? Let the peace that transcends all understanding wash over me. I thank You and praise You, In Jesus' Name, Amen.

1. Practice praying this same situation over using another Name from the list. Perhaps the Author, Shepherd, or Provider would be a good start.

2. Now choose an issue that is relevant to you, choose a Name from the chart, and practice this prayer on your own issue.

3. How do you feel now that you prayed this way?

Bible Resources Online

- YouVersion is a resource that will help you stay in the Word. It's a Bible app you can download from any app store for your mobile devices and by www.youversion.com on your computer. You can **read, listen to and watch videos of the Bible in more versions than you even knew existed**. Bible reading plans help me **read the Bible every day**. Other app capabilities include parallel versions, notes, creating verse images, and posting Bible verses on social media.

- BibleGateway is an app and great website resource for Scripture searches. It has **advanced search capabilities** that allow you to filter your search by offering a variety of specific filters such as languages, topics, match categories (such as exact phrase, all words, or any word), and side-by-side parallel versions. Download it in your app store or visit www.Biblegateway.com.

- Biblehub is for the serious Bible researcher. Just about every Bible study resource can be found in this app and website. Once you type a verse on the home search screen you find on that same results page, the Scripture in context (one verse before and one after), **parallel versions, cross-references, and commentaries.** There are simply too many features of this app to mention, but this one is great when you really want to dive into the Word and **research from many different angles.** Check out www.Biblehub.com.

- The Web Bible Encyclopedia by ChristianAnswers.net has a dictionary of **939 Names and Titles of God** with links to Scriptures that reference them. They are also distinguished by Hebrew, Greek, Aramaic, and Latin. You can use the Bible research tools below to dive into any of them on this site. http://www.christiananswers.net/dictionary/namesofgod.html

Appendix B
Salvation Prayer

⊶⊷

cts 10:36 reminds us that Jesus is the LORD of all. That means that He is the LORD of everyone, not only those who accept His gift of salvation and become children of God. It's another absolute Truth of God. Some will realize that for the first time on Judgement Day when we will all experience Romans 14:11 "As surely as I live, says the LORD, every knee will bend to Me, and every tongue will confess and give praise to God." So then, each of us will give an account of ourselves to God.

Still, for those that choose to accept the gift of salvation, we have the right to become children of God.

> John 1:12 (NIV) Yet to all who did receive him, to those who believed in his Name, He gave the right to become children of God.

We have the power to share in God's divine nature and character and truly live the lives that He has planned for us from the beginning of time.

Jeremiah 29:11-14 (NIV) [11]For I know the plans I have for you," declares the LORD, "plans to prosper you and not to harm you, plans to give you hope and a future. [12]Then you will call on me and come and pray to me, and I will listen to you. [13]You will seek me and find me when you seek me with all your heart. 14I will be found by you," declares the LORD, "and will bring you back from captivity."

If you haven't accepted Christ's gift of salvation and you are ready to do that, it's really simple. Just have a conversation with Jesus, and He will hear your heart cry. Admit that you need Jesus. Ask God for forgiveness. Believe that Jesus came to save you. Accept the free gift. Confess with your mouth that you receive the gift. Thank Him for saving you. There are no magic words to make that happen. He will accept your heartfelt prayer and send the Holy Spirit to dwell in your heart. It's that simple.

It could go something like this: Jesus, I'm tired of living my life without you. Forgive me for all my sins and for trying to do this life on my own without You. I need You to come and help me. I believe that You are who you say You are, Jesus. Thank you for offering me the way to eternal life. Come into my life now and show me how to be my best self, LORD. Thank you for sending me the Holy Spirit to show me the Way.

Once you have sincerely prayed a prayer like this, you are saved. Congratulations and welcome to the family!

Appendix C
How to Teach People to Journal

⦿⦿⦿

*I*f learning how to journal has changed your relationship with God and your life, and you want others to know how simple it is, please follow these simple steps so you can teach people how to connect with God as you can. This process can take only 30 minutes; with 15 minutes to explain it, and 15 minutes to experience God and discuss it.

1. **Induce Hunger-*Why should people want to know how to hear God's voice personally?***

    a. MOST IMPORTANTLY- Share your own story of how using this tool has changed your relationship with the Lord and changed your life. If you have a journal example you would like to share, that is usually what makes people want to try it!

    b. Ask them; Would you like to have the God who created heaven and earth speak to you by name about issues in your life; show you how to solve your problems, explain the Bible to you, give you direction, and personally heal you?

c. Explain that the Names of God are personal, such as the Bridegroom, Mighty Counselor, Friend, Defender, Provider, and Healer. Would you marry, seek counseling, trust with your secrets, and lean on when you were in crisis, someone you can't see, hear or feel? God has these Names because He showed up as these Names to people in the Bible and they personally encountered Him in these ways. So can you.

2. Normalize it- *Hearing from God is normal and easy.*

a. God created everyone to see and hear Him with the eyes and ears of their heart. If you were unable to do so, you would never have accepted Him as your Savior in the first place. God is not willing for ANY to perish, so He wired us to be able to communicate with Him.

b. The entire Bible was written using the same four keys I will teach you in a few minutes.

c. Two-thirds of the Bible came to people who heard from God and they wrote it down and one-third of the Bible came when people received messages from the Lord through dreams and visions and wrote it down. In all cases, they were using the ears and eyes of their hearts to connect with God.

d. God is the same yesterday, today, and forever (Hebrews 13:8). So, if this is how He spoke to Bible writers, He can do it now too. Even more so now that we have the Holy Spirit whose job is to endue us with the power to connect with God's nature and release His love to others. This direct access to Father God is what Jesus accomplished for us on the cross.

3. Address New Age Concern upfront- *It is different than what the New Agers do...*

a. When you ask for Jesus, you get Jesus. Matthew 7:9-11 New American Standard Bible (NASB) [9] Or what man is there among you [a]who, when his son asks for a loaf, [b]will give him a stone? [10] Or [c]if he asks for a fish, he will not give him a snake, will he? [11] If you then, being evil, know how to give good gifts to your children, how much more will your Father who is in heaven give what is good to those who ask Him?

b. New Agers seek a generalized spiritual realm and they get negative spirits.

c. We **can** know which voice-

   i. God sounds like His Names and character (fruit of the Spirit, build you up, encourage and edify, disciplines lovingly but does not condemn).

   ii. The enemy sounds like his names and character (lies, deceit, tears down, robs, steals, destroys, condemns). Condemnation speaks in generalities and results in guilt, shame, and negative identity whereas conviction is specific loving feedback and leads to repentance, healing, and restoration.

   iii. Your voice is logical and analytical and is limited to a natural world understanding.

4. **Share the Four Keys to Hearing God's Voice-** *There are four simple steps to hearing God's voice.*

a. **Quiet yourself down-** Externally and internally

b. **Fix your Eyes on Jesus**... ask and expect to see, hear, and feel from Him

c. **Tune to spontaneity-** allow the pictures, thoughts, and feelings to bubble up... don't try too hard

d. **Write down what you saw, heard, and felt,**

These steps can be seen in action in Habakkuk 2:1-2

Verse segment	How it relates to the 4 Keys
[1]I will stand on my guard post And station myself on the rampart;	He found a quiet place so he could look up to God. He was posturing his heart to speak to God Himself.
And I will keep watch to see what He will speak to me,	He was looking and listening with an expectation to hear from God personally... using the eyes and ears of his heart.
And how I may reply when I am reproved.	Habakkuk knew it would be a conversation with God. He knew that he could be able to hear what God had to say AND that he could reply.
[2]Then the LORD answered me and said,	God did reply personally.
"Record the vision and inscribe *it* on tablets, That the one who reads it may run.	God commanded Habakkuk to write down what He was going to say... writing it down is not just for you to be able to remember, but it can also be a blessing for others.

5. **Preparing for your first Jesus Encounter-**

a. Manage expectations--- God's voice sounds like your own thoughts and pictures on the screen of your mind but spontaneously and with His character... it's a bit more loving than you are usually.

b.   Practice seeing with the eyes of your heart. Close your eyes and picture your kitchen or bedroom of your house. Look around the room using the eyes of your heart. The clarity of the picture in your mind is the clarity of the image you will likely see when you go to see Jesus. So, it is not as clear as what you can see with your natural eyes, but you can still get an impression of what you are sensing.

c.   Practice hearing with the ears of your heart by closing your eyes and singing the Happy Birthday song in your mind.

d.   Some see easier and others hear easier, others get feelings. All of these are good beginnings. So, be happy with what you experience. All of us have these senses so, even if you are not experiencing all of them at first, you can ask God to give you increased sensitivity and practice. You will get better at it. So, don't despise small beginnings.

e.   Encourage them to imagine themselves as a child between the ages of 4 to 8 as this will help connect them to God with a more open heart because it activates their childlike faith.

6.   **The Special Place-** *Have a special place in your spirit where you can go and see Jesus there anytime.*

a.   This short, guided imagery will take you to a place of God's choosing for you to meet with Him. http://bit.ly/2g8v8iu

b.   How this guided imagery works, so you can facilitate something like it if you prefer.

i.   Imagine a beautiful place. For some, it will be a place that they have been where there are loving memories. For others, it is a beautiful place in general or even a supernatural place. The Lord knows exactly what place to pop into people's minds. Do not direct what this looks like. Relax and let the image pop into your mind. God speaks in your language, so even if it seems strange at first, go with it.

ii. Wake up and activate the Right-brain by asking them to see, hear, smell, and feel this place, left, front, right, up, and down. Speak it slowly enough for them to take in some details. This part is to make sure they are waking up their spiritual senses even before we introduce Jesus to the scene. Again, do not tell them what to see here, just tell them to look, and listen.

iii. Then ask them to turn around and see Jesus walking toward them. He has a smile on His face. When He approaches, He hugs them. This is specifically, so they see Jesus as His loving character.

iv. The first question that we recommend that they ask Jesus is "How do You feel about Me"? Then, completely take your hand off the wheel and let Jesus take it from there.

c.   Give them time. Eight to ten minutes is usually a good amount of time. Then ask them to share their experience. If you are giving them the link above and they are not doing it now, schedule a time to review their first journal. This increases the likelihood that they do it.

d.   Encourage them in their experience. This was a REAL Jesus encounter, not a figment of their imagination. Tell them that they can go back to the special place ANYTIME and Jesus will be there for them again.

About Dr. Patty Sadallah

atty Sadallah has a Doctorate of Ministry in Christian Leadership/Discipleship from Christian Leadership University. She is passionate about showing people how to encounter God personally so they may live their lives through faith in Jesus through the power of the Holy Spirit. Her mission is to bring the message of the realness of God and the practicality of intimacy and relationship with God to the masses by incorporating media in her messages.

Dr. Sadallah is a Professor at Christian Leadership University serving master's and doctoral students. Additionally, she leads the Spirit Life Circle mentored coaching ministry offered internationally through Communion with God Ministries. Additionally, she leads the Spirit Life Workshops Ministry practically facilitating Jesus encounters that aid people to better connect with God for healing and activation of their callings.

She has more than 35 years of experience serving faith-based nonprofit organizations and small groups as an Organization Development Consultant, Coach, Facilitator, Trainer, and Bible Study Leader.

Patty and George have been married since 1986 and have three lovely daughters: Jamael, Leah, and Noelle. Jamael and her husband Nick have three sweet grandchildren.

Books by Dr. Patty Sadallah

*D*r. Patty Sadallah has authored the award-winning and recently updated book ***Clips that Move Mountains 2ⁿᵈ Edition,*** a Discipleship book that includes 23 film clips, and ***Journey to the Abundant Christian Life,*** its Bible study companion.

Additionally, ***How to Live a Worry-Free Life: Just ask Jesus Book 1.*** Look for more in this series after the completion of the Experience Jesus series.

The **Experience Jesus Series** includes 4 books and their accompanying **Experience Jesus Journals**.

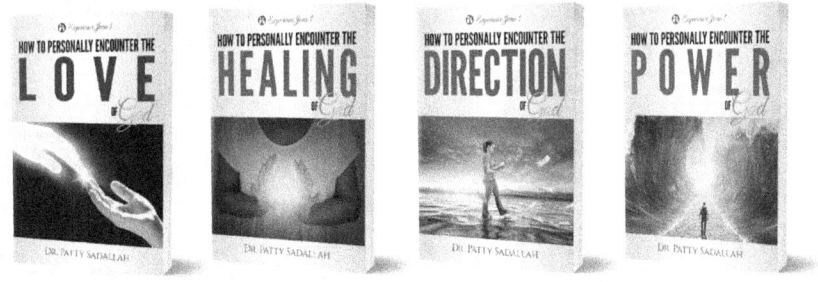

Book 1: *How to Encounter the LOVE of God; and the Experience the LOVE of God Journal*

Book 2: *How to Encounter the HEALING of God; and the Experience the HEALING of God Journal*

Book 3: *How to Encounter the DIRECTION of God and the Experience the DIRECTION of God Journal and,*

Book 4: *How to Encounter the POWER of God. (Coming 2023)*

All books and other downloadable resources are available on **https://PattySadallah.com/shop**

They can also be found on **Amazon.com** and **BarnesAndNoble. com** The easiest way to find Dr. Sadallah's books is to **simply search "Patty Sadallah"** on these bookstore websites.

Check out more about each book and the other ministry opportunities by visiting her website at **www.PattySadallah.com**

Dr. Sadallah is available for speaking, teaching, and facilitation related to discipleship for individuals, small groups, organizations, and multi-organizational planning needs. God Bless you!

Patty Sadallah

www.ingramcontent.com/pod-product-compliance
Lightning Source LLC
Chambersburg PA
CBHW060527150626
46553CB00023B/311